DEDICATION

*"I dedicate this book to the Christian Body of Believers who sense the urgency to search the depths of God's purpose for their lives on the earth. As you read this book, I pray you receive the revelation of who God is and allow Him to stir your spiritual passion to walk in the fullness of who He desires to be in you. I pray you catch the vision of our Sovereign, Omniscient, and Transcendent God who spoke into creation those three powerful words **"Let there be"** allowing everything in our past, present and future to yield in obedience. Finally, I pray you receive the wisdom to agree with what Our Father is continuously declaring regarding His children and His church. Our Father spoke to our end from the beginning and His words continue to reverberate throughout our existence in time and space. His expectation of us is Great!"*

Terry Marr

ACKNOWLEDGEMENTS

I take this time to acknowledge the many people who have been instrumental in assisting me in writing this book. Thank you, L.C. Marr, for your love, devotion to me, and faithfulness to the call of God on your life. I am so grateful Father God placed us together. I thank you for believing in me and standing beside me through everything we have had to endure over the years.

Thanks to my spiritual coaches, Pastor Daniel and Sheila Rhodes for the sessions of counseling and words of encouragement you share so freely. My husband and I love you so much.

Thank you, New Life Community Church, for praying for me through this writing project and for allowing L.C. and me to be your pastors.

Thank you Mosal Morszart for your insight in imagery.

Thank you Father God for trusting m[e] body of believers for such a time as this. I love you!

CONTENTS

What You Can Expect From This Book

Romans 8:18-23 states,

For I consider that the sufferings of this present time are not worthy to be compared with the glory which shall be revealed in us. 19 For the earnest expectation of the creation eagerly waits for the revealing of the sons of God. 20 For the creation was subjected to futility, not willing, but because of Him who subjected it in hope; 21 because the creation itself also will be delivered from the bondage of corruption into the glorious liberty of the children of God. 22 For we know that the whole creation groans and labors with birth pangs together until now. 23 Not only that, but we also who have the first fruits of the Spirit, even we ourselves groan within ourselves, eagerly waiting for the adoption the redemption of our body (NKJV).

I am compelled to write this book for the body of Believers who are ready to walk in the power and presence of the Lord Jesus. Those who are determined to forget those things that are behind and press for those things that are before that lead to developing the Mind of Christ.

Warning: This book is not for the Sunday Morning Christian who is satisfied with just knowing he or she will miss hell one day. It is not for those who are satisfied with someone else telling them what the Word of God says because they are too lazy to read it for themselves.

This book is for the Marys, Abrahams, Elijahs, Davids, Joshuas, Moseses, Daniels, Rahabs, Peters and Pauls who are ready to accept the clarion call to action. Not the call to Hollywood to become the next great wonder, but the call to stand on the walls of the cities and declare Jesus as Lord and Savior; not with lip service, but in the anointing that breaks yokes by the demonstration of the Holy Spirit of God working through us.

This book is designed to allow those who hunger and thirst after Righteousness to stay in the face of God until we can no longer recognize ourselves as mere church goers, but have willingly put on the whole armor of God and purposefully walk in the Righteousness of Our God. This book will share the story of how the God of all creation sought us out in the beginning and claimed us as His own, not only conquerors in the army of God, but more than conquerors. It is the story of how Father God desires to transform our lives into the image He has designed, allowing us to agree with Him in tearing down strong holds and spreading the Love of God and the Message of Jesus throughout the earth. This is the story of how our continuous search for Him will leads to a closer and deeper relationship with the One and Only, Wise and True God of all creation. This is the story of the path that leads us into the face of Father God who created, formed, called and chose us to be 'The Lamb's Bride'. It is the love story of us who belong to Him, the One with whom we have to do. This is the story of Our Triune God, and His desire to draw us deeper into Himself and to encourage us to search the depths of the Living God. During our search, we will get to know the God who has called us out of darkness into His glorious light and discover His expectations of us. We will learn how to stir up the gifts given us by the Holy Spirit and how to follow His leading as we will learn to yield to the potter's wheel of the Father and with His permission, finally, manifest as the sons of God!

Terry Marr

Preface

I have always believed in God. I have never considered Him as an option or a second thought; His presence has always been as real to me as the air I breathe. Growing up as a "little colored girl" in the 1950's in Memphis, Tennessee, going to church on Sundays and to Bible study through the week were a given. I still remember how excited I would get after dinner when I would walk with my siblings to choir rehearsal on Saturday afternoon to our neighborhood church. Singing songs to the Lord and finding ways to please Him summed up my life back then, and the only dilemmas I had to contend with at that age were getting my chores done in a timely manner so I could watch the Billy Graham crusades on our oversized black and white television by 6 pm. Life was so uncomplicated then, and between television shows like *Leave it to Beaver* and *The Flintstones*, in prime time, what more could a child ask for?

I grew up in a Christian home, my philosophy of God was one I had learned from listening to the grown-ups during family time as they sat in the lawn chairs around the big oak tree in the backyard, fighting off mosquitoes and fireflies. Sunday morning service at the neighborhood church was not only a time to hear the choir sing but to sit and listen to the preacher talk about how we were all going to see Jesus "one of these ole days." Unlike most of the children I dealt with, I believed everything I heard about God in the bible, so much so, I had memorized every biblical story and loved to visualize Jesus, Himself, sitting and talking to me about the New Testament parables. The Word of God seemed to come alive in me and I often found myself in my room with the lights off, talking to God about my day and telling Him how much I loved Him. No matter what was going on in my life, I knew if I could just get home to my Jesus, He would make everything right again. Yes, I was living in a Jesus bubble and I loved it! Nothing bad could touch me there and if I had any say in the matter, nothing

7

ever would.

As the eleventh of twelve siblings, I enjoyed a well-rounded and structured life. My Dad worked for the Tennessee Valley Authority and my Mom was a stay home disciplinarian for our very lively household. One would think coming from such a large family one would never feel isolated or alone, but by the age of five I would find myself playing by myself, a lot. I had developed this condition called "trichotillomania" that brought on irresistible urges to pull my hair out from the root. Of course back in the late fifty's we did not know there was a name for it; therefore my mother would just tell her friends I had a nervous condition that caused me to have bald spots in my scalp. When the condition first developed, my Mom would spank and scold me, all to no avail. When that didn't work, she would talk to me to see if I knew "why I was doing this to myself?" I could see how much it upset her, but God knows I could not stop. Throughout the days and years following, I would hear my Mother praying to God about me. We never saw our Mother's tears, but they were there when she sought answers from God for the troubles that plagued her children. It was while seeking for answers to this nervous disorder my Mom noticed something else which seemed to cause the embarrassment of my balding scalp to pale in comparison. The time I was spending with my Jesus was developing into the manifestation of gifts of the Holy Spirit of God.

My Mom first took notice when, at the age of five and six, I would go to her and deliver messages from God to questions she alone knew she had ask of Him. I did not think anything about what was happening to me because I did not recognize it as strange or unusual. I had been able to hear the voice of God clearly for the longest time and it was only natural that, eventually, it would be noticed by someone who could help me understand it to be a spiritual gift from God. That someone was my Mom. For years I had spoken to my siblings and others about things God had said to me without much of a reaction, but when I begin to share with my Mom information regarding sicknesses that were going on with her friends, troubles that were happening in her family and challenges on Dad's job; she recognized God was pouring out his gifts upon the most unlikely of her children. From that moment on, my Mom stopped praying and fixating on my natural appearance and begin to pray with me explaining the importance of getting to know the God who is the giver of such gifts. I looked forward to the time she would share with me teaching me about the bible and directing me in the things of God. During our time together and her instructing me in the things of God, the nervous disorder soon disappeared never to return; thus started my journey of knowledge, wisdom, understanding and revelation of the Only Wise and True Living God and His Righteous Rule over all things.

THE VISION OF THE LAMB'S HEAD

At the age of 18 years old, I met my husband, L.C. Marr, at a tent revival. I had been reared in the Church of God in Christ. He was a Baptist junior deacon, and before long we fell in love and were married. We both loved God and wanted to please Him in every way. L. C. became an over the road trucker, and I went to school to become a registered nurse. Shortly after my graduation from nursing school, L.C. came to me and announced the Lord had told him to start a church in the Memphis area. He was already preaching in our home church, so I was not surprised God would call him to pastor. What did surprise me was this meant God was calling me to be a pastor's wife. Neither of us had had any formal ministerial training and had no idea where or how to start a ministry. We checked with other pastors and ministries, but they stated they could not help us unless we agreed to become a part of their organization or denomination. L.C. had already mentioned God was not leading him to join any denomination, so we turned to the God who called us and promised to trust and depend on Him for all our needs. This, too, was not surprising to me because I had already begin to feel the Lord teaching us to walk by faith and trust in Him with all of our hearts. The first thing I did was revert back to what I had done as a child, pray without ceasing. My husband and I had no idea what God was after, but we were determined to give Him all we had. As with most new beginnings, starting the work of the Lord was challenging because we were both working full time and before long had a growing family of our own.

One evening while seeking the Lord, I began to pray about the ministry and ask the Lord to keep us on course and in His will. Keep in mind, during these days the Lord would not let us affiliate with other churches or even go to them for advice. It was as though He deliberately kept us isolated. As I began to worship the Lord in my prayer closet, the strangest thing happened.

I was on my knees praying with the lights off when suddenly I felt as though someone had placed a warm blanket over me. The room began to illuminate as a white screen unfolded before me. There appeared a man's hand drawing on the screen in such a way I found myself holding my breath awaiting and anticipating every moment as it unfolded. Before long I recognized the drawing to be that of the head of a lamb. Although it was a drawing, I stared in awe as the drawing came to life and the Lamb turned to look at me. It was then I noticed there were hundreds of tiny markers all over the lamb's chins. I also noticed about ten marks on its cheeks and four marks on its right ear and three on its left ear. While watching this vision, I became aware I could see everything but I could not move. I was as though I was restricted in movement but quite aware of what was happening before me. Suddenly I heard myself say, "Lord, what are you showing me? Why is the lamb's chin covered with marks?"

The Lord said, "The marks on the chin represent areas of familiarity for some of my people. These are areas established and passed down to them by their father's and mother's and declared to be where they and those coming behind them can always find me; therefore they continue to migrate to this area of familiarity and hope. They have congregated themselves together in clusters to draw upon "passed down religious beliefs" of others while searching for strength and confirmation of who they think I am. Like their parents before them, many have seen me work in certain areas of their lives and they have become very comfortable living in those areas of limited knowledge. The markers represent areas of security and comfort for them. In these man-made havens of confidence, they believe they are experiencing my best when it comes to certain kinds of healing, bits of financial prosperity, and some deliverances in these areas. They have learned to trust me as long as I stay within the confines of what they have seen and heard and believe. They think these limited encounters they have had with me define who I am. No more . . . no less."

I asked, "Lord, what about the markers on the cheeks?"

The Lord said, "These are those who are slowly venturing out to explore me at higher levels. They know I have more for them, but they are unwilling to go too far without the backup support of men or other denominational groups."

I then asked, "Lord tell me about the higher marks on the ears."

Jesus said, "Every now and then, I find someone who is able and willing to believe against belief, not because they have seen me do it before or even because they have heard of it being done before, but simply because I said it. With no point of reference, they move in obedience for my good pleasure."

He begin to minister to me about the Virgin Mary, who was willing to conceive the Christ child against all belief or customs of her day. While still a virgin and with no guarantee from the angel that her family and friends would believe or even support her choice, she yielded her will to the will of the Father. Despite the shame, Mary agreed with God; not because she had seen it done before, but simply because the Lord instructed her to.

The Lord spoke to me about Abraham who left everything he had just to become the father of many nations, simply because God instructed him to. He went on reminding me of Samuel, Joseph, and Moses. He said, "I need someone who will allow me to show myself strong; someone who will allow me to show my versatility. Instead of expecting me to use the same floor plan, building materials and blueprints I used for someone else, allow me to build and fashion my house, my choir, my church and my ministry my way. I need my people to trust me. I need someone who is not afraid to wait . . . on Me."

The words He spoke to me penetrated my very soul. Slowly,

the screen disappeared and the room was once again darkened, but I continued to feel the warmth of the spiritual blanket around me. When I came to myself, I was still on my knees in my prayer closet and I heard myself repeating over and over again with tears streaming down my face, "You've found a people . . . You've found us . . . You've found me."

Since that time, the God I met and talked about and to as a child is now bigger and more amazing than ever. My perceptions of Him are so much greater than I ever knew possible. My life is now filled with numerous visions, dreams and spiritual gifts that, only, the God of all creation could allow to be revealed. Of all of the gifts my Heavenly Father has bestowed upon me, it is the ability to teach the Word of God that I am the most grateful. Through this gift He allows me to share the simple truths and revelations about Him- not only what He does but who He has revealed to me He wants to be in us. With every year, my anticipation regarding the Lamb's Head vision begins to heighten. No matter how difficult or challenging the journey appears, I always remember what the Lord stated He requires and I know I will not leave this earth without fulfilling that promise to allow Him to take me higher than I ever thought possible.

THE BREAK-IN

Visions such as the *Lamb's Head* are not sent of God to enter-tain us, but to prepare us for what is ahead. Before the vision, I had led a very sheltered life where my mother and father had been my protec-tors and providers. Now I found myself newly married with children of my own and faced with the uncertainties of holding down a full time job, learning the role of a mother and wife and starting a fledgling ministry. I was also under the impression God must have allowed me to have visions and dreams because He was requiring things of me that were supernatural; therefore I needed to be ready to perform some great feat for the Body of Christ. "How can God use me," I wondered, "when I was so fearful, self-conscious and uncertain about myself?" With these thoughts came the pressure to try to make myself into this anointed saint of God ready to walk water at the drop of a hat. Isn't it amazing how we freak ourselves out thinking everything is about us? No wonder, so many of us are medicated on tranquilizers and anti-depressants. It took me years to recognize everything in my life was established by God long before I arrived on the earth. The book of Jeremiah 1:4 says it this way,

Then the word of the Lord came to me, saying; 5"Before I formed you in the womb I knew you; Before you were born I sanctified you; I ordained you a prophet to the nations"(NKJV).

According to this scripture, God had already declared my end long before I began. The same goes for all of us who belong to Him. Our biggest job is to stop stressing over what we will be and just, become. But in the becoming we are to learn to yield to the leading of the Holy Spirit.

A year or so after finishing nursing school, I was working at one of the city hospitals in Memphis, Tennessee, on the 11-7 shift. My husband and I were both working full time and our children were

16 and 9 years old. This particular night my husband was out of town working and I was not feeling well, so I called in sick. After making sure the children were in bed I did a little reading and went to bed myself. (For about a year before this incident occurred, I had been led of the Holy Spirit to establish a special prayer and bible reading time each day. During these times with the Lord I had developed an ear to hear Him and began to feel very comfortable with His promptings). After I had been asleep for a few hours, I began to feel the presence of the Holy Spirit at my bedside. I was not surprised at His presence because it had become a common occurrence over the last year, but because I was so sleepy I did not respond to Him in my usual way. Then I heard Him say, "Pray." For some reason I felt so exhausted and could only muster up a few "thank you Jesus" and a halfhearted "bless my children and husband." Before long, I was fast asleep once more.

Then I felt the presence even stronger as His request became more urgent, "Pray now!" This time I sat straight up in bed and reached for my Bible. Now feeling the urgency of the moment, I threw back the covers to get to the bathroom where I could cry out to God. Before I could place my feet on the floor, I heard the peaceful voice of the Holy Spirit say, "Do not get up . . . just sit still and pray." In a whispered voice, I began to pray for my husband because he was on the road at work, then I prayed for the children and then I began to pray in my heavenly language allowing the Holy Spirit to guide my utterances. Before long a calmness enveloped me as I felt the peace of the Lord all around me. In the midst of all of this, I heard the bedroom door creak open and in came a man who I had never seen before in my life. With the lights in the room off, all I could see was his silhouette through the ambient light of the moon streaming from the open window shades. I noticed he was an average sized man with a bandana like scarf around his head. He was dressed in black and slowly moved from the doorway to the foot of my bed. Realizing this man had just broken into our home, I heard myself say, "Who are you and what do you want?" With all the arrogance he could muster he answered, "Don't you worry about who I am, you just sit there and I will take what I want." I watched him as he slowly walked around my bedroom picking up my belongings and examining them, slipping into his pockets those items he deemed worthy of his heist. I continued to watch as he picked up my purse, dumped it out on the bed and combed through its contents. All while he was strutting through my house, he was speaking words of fear and intimidation meant to remind me he was in control of the situation.

(Now you must understand, I am the same person that a year ago ran crying and screaming from my house because I saw a mouse in the kitchen)!

All while I am sitting there watching him, I could feel the presence of the Holy Spirit all over me. It was as though I was being infused with power from on High. Suddenly, without considering the consequences of my actions or the graveness of these circumstances, I found myself standing on my bed shouting at this intruder at the top of my voice.

"Get Out of My House . . . This Family Belongs to God . . . This House and Everything In It Belongs to God! Get Yourself Out Of This House Now In The Name of Jesus While You Still Can!!!!!!"

Although I was speaking, it was not my voice I was hearing. Then I saw this stranger look up at me on the bed and with a look of terror drop my belongings and ran from the room. (I don't know what the Lord allowed this man to see standing on that bed, but it was not a woman in a nightgown). The next thing I knew, I jumped off the bed and began to chase him through the house. No gun, no knife, no mace . . . Just Holy Ghost Power! When I got to the kitchen on the other side of the house I realized I had lost him. I called out to my children to wake up and help me get this man out of our house. Thinking he may have the car keys, I instructed everyone to run out to the car and sit on the car so he could not get away. Meanwhile, I sent my daughter back into the house to get the phone so I could call 911. In all of the excitement, I had just assumed the intruder had run out of the house, but I was mistaken. He was still in the house when I sent my daughter back in to get the phone, but God was with us. She ran into the kitchen got the telephone and the intruder did not show his face again. She was able to get the telephone and get back to me without any problem. It wasn't until the police were doing their investigation that I was told how the intruder had hidden in the house until he knew we were outside then sneaked out of the house through a window and climbed over the fence in the back yard to make his escape.

During the police investigation, we realized this man had been all through our house. Everything we owned had been packed up, wrapped up and stacked in the den of our home. One of the officers showed me how the man had left all of his break-in tools, his crack pipe and crack outside on the patio along with a snack. During the walk through, the policemen scolded me for taking such a chance with my life. Even then I could not explain to them what had happened because somehow I really didn't think they would have understood. By this time, my husband had made it to the house. I noticed he was looking at me strangely and standing off to the side. After a while he tried to approach me, and I told him, "Oh, Baby, don't worry about me, I'm fine." After the police had completed their report, I told everybody to go back to bed and get some sleep. Again my husband, stayed up and sat at the edge of the bed watching me sleep.

Several hours later, I woke up screaming and shaking. I looked up and there my husband was holding me. "What are you doing sitting here," I asked, "Oh," he replied. "I was waiting for my wife to come back because the woman I saw when I got here was someone I did not know even existed. As soon as you fell asleep, I realized you must have been under some kind of anointing because the Terry I love and know, so well, would never have been that cool in the midst of a break-in. I figured when the anointing wore off and reality set in, you just might be in need of a hug or two."

I thank God for Jesus, my husband and for the Power of the Holy Spirit. I pondered the words my husband had spoken to me. In the midst of this ordeal, he was looking for *Clark Kent,* but because of the encounter with the Holy Spirit of God he witnessed *Super Man,* or should I say, *Super Saint* better known as a *son of God.* The God of all creation took the time to send his Angels to watch over the things that concern me in the time of danger and trouble. This situation and deliverance is the way all of us are to expect to live when we belong to God. Our Father promised, before we call, He will answer! Look what He says regarding Saul in the Old Testament,

1 Samuel 10:6,

Then the Spirit of the Lord will come upon you, and you will prophesy with them and be turned into another man (NKJV).

1 John 3:2 says,

Beloved, now are we the sons of God, and it doth not yet appear what we shall be: but we know that, when he shall appear, we shall be like him; for we shall see him as he is (KJV).

And what about Psalms 91:1, 5-7,

1 He who dwells in the secret place of the Most High Shall abide under the shadow of the Almighty. 2 I will say of the Lord, "He is my refuge and my fortress; My God, in Him I will trust."

5 You shall not be afraid of the terror by night, Nor of the arrow that flies by day, 6 Nor of the pestilence that walks in darkness, Nor of the destruction that lays waste at noonday. 7 A thousand may fall at your side, and ten thousand at your right hand; But it shall not come near you (NKJV).

BUT, I'M MORE THAN THAT!

A few weeks ago I decided to visit the children's ministry at our Memphis site, New Life Community Church, during the Sunday school hour. In the toddler's classes, I was a bit disturbed by the comprehension regarding the size and potential of the God we serve. After attentively listening to the teacher minister the story of the creation, I saw a group of eager toddlers demonstrating to their class how God created the animals, trees and all of creation. Working in silence and with as much concentration as three year olds can muster, the children broke off pieces of Play Dough and gently formed each creature one by one. Afterwards they placed their creations together in a box labeled "Earth" and proceeded to demonstrate their perception of how God placed the sun, moon and stars into space. With the most precious smiles and grins on each face, they hurriedly began to show me their creations for inspection and approval. I stood there praising the children for their efforts as the teacher placed a movie into the DVD player and the children scurried to watch the 3D bible study presentation of the morning. While standing there watching this familiar scene, I heard the Holy Spirit speak to me.

"Why are you teaching them a one dimensional side of me? They see the world in 3D, but I am considered a one dimensional God. It is time to teach them the God you know me to be. They see me as God in an ancient book with black and white pages or in a children's book with painted-colored cartoon figures. When they close the book- they no longer see me. Get Me off the pages and allow Me to become real to them. Teach them my **'Transcendence'.**"

Before leaving the room, I looked at the faces of the children and recognized how their entire countenance had changed while watching the video. They live in a world full of super heroes who fly across the screen moving in and out of dimensions, while fighting villains and saving the universe. Then they come to church, and we teach them the laws or commandments of God without teaching them who God- really- is. Wow, I knew exactly what God was saying to me. All of my life I have experienced a multi-dimensional, multi-purposeful, omniscient, omnipresent, omnipotent, sovereign God, yet because I was unsure everyone was capable of understanding the mysteries of His ways and His acts, I had toned down my teaching to help others relate to Him on their level. What a trick of the enemy. How presumptuous of me. In other words, I had tried to become their Holy Spirit revealing God to them as I thought they could understand. Yes, there are mysteries in God, but it is not my job to decide because a person is unchurched or younger or older than myself what they can handle or even are willing to believe. My job is to teach and preach the truths from the Word of God just as He has revealed them to me through His Holy Spirit. I believe this is a word for many of us in the ministry. We are to teach and preach Our God in the Body of Christ until He is recognizable to all who are called according to His purpose. We are to teach the power, majesty, glory and sovereignty of "Him with whom we have to do." (Hebrews 4:13) KJV. Don't try to explain Him; that is the work of Holy Spirit.

But the Comforter, which is the Holy Ghost, whom the Father will send in my name He shall teach you all things, and bring all things to your remembrance, whatsoever I have said unto you. (John 14: 26).

All through the morning worship at New Life, I found myself thinking about what the Holy Spirit had said to me, *"Get God off the pages and allow Him to become a reality in the hearts of the people."* As soon as service was dismissed, I was on my way home to my prayer closet to seek the Lord.

On the way home, I remembered an incident that had happened to me during a visit to an out of town revival a friend of ours was conducting. He had invited an evangelist whom I was unfamiliar with but I was looking forward to the fellowship and ministry. The message was timely and the atmosphere was charged with anticipation as the evangelist begin to minister to the congregation through the gifts of the Spirit. My husband and I were sitting on the second row and were in ear shot of everything the evangelist was saying to the people coming up for the altar call. Suddenly, the evangelist stopped in his tracks and begin to gaze at the people in the seats. He walked over to one of the men in the front row and asked him to stand. Then, by the power of the Holy Spirit, the evangelist spoke into the life of this man in such a way that the man fell to his knees and begin to cry out to God. With tears running down his face, the man thanked the preacher for obeying the voice of God and giving him the answer to a petition he had had before the Lord for weeks. The man then begin to sob uncontrollably, but the joy of the Lord was all over him. Just to watch this man get his break-through made me rejoice in the wonderment of our Lord. The words the evangelist had spoken to him were precise and specific, and the atmosphere was charged with even more expectancy. I remember whispering to the Lord, "You are so awesome, thank you for your mighty power." Then I heard the Holy Spirit say to me, **"But I'm more than that."** Next the evangelist walked over to this elderly woman and began to tell her every sickness she had dealt with in her adult life. He shared with her that there was a demon assigned to keep her sick and distracted from the things God had ordained for her to walk in. Suddenly, the evangelist laid his hand on the lady's head. She hit the floor like a sack of potatoes and came up rejoicing and running around the sanctuary. The church broke out in corporate praise. Once again I whispered to the Holy Spirit, "You are amazing, thank you for knowing what we need and showing us how to receive."

Once again I heard Him say, **"But I'm more than that."** Then I heard the Holy Spirit say to me, "Think of the greatest thing you can imagine me doing. Think of the mightiest, most powerful event you have known happen in all the universe."

I sat there in silence as my mind drifted to the Red Sea experience, the walls of Jericho and the resurrection of Our Lord Jesus and when I began to form the words to answer the Lord, I looked up and the Evangelist was standing over me. I heard him say to me with a huge smile on his face, **"Yes, but He is more than that."** In my heart I knew this preacher did not know of the conversation I was having with my Lord, but God allowed him to speak into my hearing what only I knew God was saying at that time. Needless to say, that moment changed me forever.

IN THE BEGINNING

Finally, I pulled in to our driveway and could still hear the words the Lord had spoken to me, *"Teach them my transcendence".* Upon entering the house, I went to the den and grabbed the dictionary from the bookshelf.

According to the *Webster's New World College Dictionary (ed. 4)* transcend means

- To climb over

- To go beyond the limits of; overstep; exceed

- To be superior to; surpass; excel

- To be separate from or beyond

Transcendent means

- Transcending; surpassing; excelling; extraordinary

- Beyond the limits of possible experience

- Existing apart from the material universe; (example: said of God)

My heart began to beat faster as my expectations of God began to grow. Like a child on his first day in school, I rushed to my prayer closet and immediately sensed the presence of the Lord. With Bible in hand, I could sense the Holy Spirit standing before me and once again I found myself in a heightened state of anticipation. I have often felt my spirit man being led by the Holy Spirit, but this time something more seemed to be happening. It was as though I was in a classroom for one and the Holy Spirit was teaching, guiding and answering me all at the same time. Then it happened. With the Bible turned to the book of Genesis chapter one, I perceived in the scripture our Father God standing in the distance in all His spender surrounded by light and glory. Then the scriptures ministered to me saying,

"In the beginning God created the heaven and the earth. And the earth was without form, and void; and darkness was upon the face of the deep. And the Spirit of God moved upon the face of the waters. And God said, "Let there be light; and there was light" Genesis 1:1-3 (KJV).

With the scriptures before me, the Holy Spirit continued to guide me through the genesis of creation showing me the significance and power of every word spoken by Our Omniscient Father into the atmosphere. I gazed at every verse that began with the words *"**And God said,**"* recognizing how each creation and creature spoken into existence eagerly submitted to His voice. With every word spoken by Our Father proceeded life, purpose, direction and submission to His desires. I perceived how the Father open His mouth and out of his mouth came the words ". . . ***Let there be,***" and attached to the words spoken by God came "The Word". **It was Jesus in Spirit form.** (Staring in awe as the scriptures began to come alive in my hand, I understood how each time Father God opened his mouth, Jesus parts the Father's lips and moved through the outer limits of space to do the bidding of the Father. With every word God said, Jesus appears as the Word being spoken by God, and as the words were **said by God**, Jesus created what God said to the Father's specifications. Jesus did not deviate from what the Father said. Just as it was spoken, the request was structured and fashioned to the Father's specifications and will. I felt the Bible coming alive inside me. Could it be that simple, yet that mysterious?

Then Holy Spirit brought to my remembrance how John 4:24 states,

"God is Spirit, they that worship Him must worship Him in spirit and in truth" (KJV).

Then He took me to St. John 14: 10 where Jesus said:

24

"Don't you believe that I am in the Father and the Father is in me? The words I speak are not my own, but my Father who lives in me does his work through me" (New International Version).

Then, I remembered what Jesus said in St John 8:28,

"When ye have lifted up the Son of man, then shall ye know that I am he, and that I do nothing of myself; but as my Father has taught me, I speak these things" (KJV).

I watched in wonder as the Bible came alive in my hands with the Father, Son and the Holy Spirit as the authors, directors and special effects composers. **Father spoke it and Jesus created it and the Holy Spirit hovered over it to perform it**. All three persons, in each other in total and complete unity.

John 17:21,

. . . that they all may be one, as You, Father, are in Me, and I in You; that they also may be one in Us, that the world may believe that You sent Me (NKJV).

I read in awe as the Father spoke the Word and it was so. Unlike the elementary teachings I had retained in my youth, the Father, through the scripture, was showing me how everything was spoken, created and performed in concert, **"in the beginning."** I saw the heavens and the earth past, present and future come to life all at the same time. Like a sovereign conductor directing an eternal orchestra, the entire creation was before me. This was no one dimensional God with an assembly line piping one creature out at a time, but an All-Consuming, Transcendent God spilling out His thoughts, plans, designs, purposes and perfections upon a waiting canvass. Suddenly, it all seemed to make sense. St John 1:1 says regarding Jesus:

"In the beginning was the Word (Jesus) and the Word was with God, and the Word was God. 2 The same was in the beginning with God. 3

All things were made by him and without him was not anything made that was made. 4 In him was life; and the life was the light of men. 5 And the light shineth in darkness, and the darkness comprehended it not" (KJV).

Before I could ask the next question, Holy Spirit guided me to St. John 14: 8-11 (NIV)

8 Phillip said, "Lord, show us the Father, and we will be satisfied." 9 Jesus replied, "Have I been with you all this time, Philip, and yet you still don't know who I am? Anyone who has seen me has seen the Father! So why are you asking me to show him to you? 10 Don't you believe that I am in the Father and the Father is in me? The words I speak are not my own, but my Father who lives in me does his work through me. 11 Just believe that I am in the Father and the Father is in me. Or at least believe because of the work you have seen me do."

Hebrews 1: 1-3 states in the NIV,

*Long ago God spoke many times, and in many ways to our ancestors through the prophets. 2 And now in these final days, he has spoken to us through his Son. God promised everything to the Son as an inheritance, **and through the Son he created the universe**. 3 The Son radiates God's own glory and expresses the very character of God and he sustains everything by the mighty power of his command. When he had cleansed us from our sins, he sat down in the place of honor at the right hand of the majestic God in heaven.*

With tears rolling down my face, I held tightly to the Bible, as the Holy Spirit continued to minister to me the will of the Father. Not only did the Father say it and Jesus create it, but with every word came instructions to the creature and the creation. Genesis 1:20 – 22 says,

"And God said, Let the waters bring forth abundantly the moving creature that hath life, and fowl that may fly above the earth in the

open firmament of heaven. 21 And God created great whales, and every living creature that moveth, which the waters brought forth abundantly, after their kind, and every winged fowl after his kind; and God saw that it was good. 22 And God blessed them saying, Be fruitful and multiply, and fill the waters in the seas, and let fowl multiply in the earth. 24 And God said, Let the earth bring forth the living creature after his kind cattle, and creeping thing and beast of the earth after his kind; and it was so" (KJV).

Let's continue reading in the New International Version (NIV):

*25 God made all sorts of wild animals, livestock, and small animals, each able to produce offspring of the same kind. And God saw that it was good. 26 Then God said, "Let us make human beings (in the King James Version it says, "Let us make man – in the Hebrew the interpretation is Adam) in our image, to be like us. They will reign over (have dominion KJV) the fish in the sea, the birds in the sky, the livestock, all the wild animals **on the earth,** and the small animals that scurry along the ground." 27 So God created human beings in his own image In the image of God he created them; male and female he created them. 28 Then God blessed them and said, "Be fruitful and multiply. Fill the earth and govern it. Reign over the fish in the sea the birds in the sky, and all the animals that scurry along the ground." 29 Then God said, "Look! I have given you every seed-bearing plant **throughout the earth** and all the fruit trees for your food. 30 And I have given every green plant as food for all the wild animals, the birds in the sky, and the small animals that scurry along the ground-everything that has life," And that is what happened.*

Our Father's plans and purposes for us was so well thought out and orchestrated that God said it one time and never had to go back and create anything again.

When I was a child, I used to hate to get jig-saw puzzles for presents. Just the thought of knowing how much time it would take to put it together was "down right depressing." Looking at the pretty picture on the box made me think I could get it done without too much trouble, but once I poured out the pieces and recognized how tiny and intricate each piece appeared, I knew I was not up for the task. I would often invite other siblings to help me tackle this giant, but after a few minutes of staring and searching for pieces of the puzzle (you knew were invisible to the human eye) they, too, grew discouraged and walked away. Periodically, I would go back again and look at the puzzle and try forcing pieces together, but no matter how acceptable it may appear on the table, once I tried to move it to another canvas, the whole thing would fall apart.

As I look back on those times, I realize that even then the Lord was preparing me for my journey through this life with Him. I began to sense the Holy Spirit guiding me through the mysteries of how Our Great Triune God works on the behalf of His children to bring about His purposes in our lives. Like a child with a brand new jig-saw puzzle, we think we know what we need to make our lives work. We go to self-help sessions to find the answers to life's questions only to discover what worked for one person does not necessarily fit in your own life. Our lives were never meant to be frustrating and chaotic, with us running around in circles trying to figure out where all of the pieces fit. Father God did not just hand us a box of broken puzzle pieces and say, "Just figure it out and get back to me later." We are not pieces on a chess board with God waiting for us to check out. Our Father is not the warden of our prisons, but the Lover of our souls. The Word of God states "In the beginning" we are fearfully and wonderfully made and every moment of every day of our lives God is trying to get us to trust in Him, leaning not to our own understanding. Sure, we sometimes come up with answers on our own that seem to solve the puzzle for a moment, but before long we recognize every time we try to move with that plan the entire picture falls apart. Just like scattered pieces of the jig-saw puzzle, our well organized, Omniscient, Omnipotent, Sovereign God patiently waits for us to yield to His creative purposes and plans for our lives. To understand where you fit in the scheme of things you must consult and trust the Creator.

Proverbs 3:5-6 states,

Trust in the Lord with all your heart, and lean not on your own understanding; 6 In all your ways acknowledge Him, And He shall direct your paths (NKJV).

UNDERSTANDING THE TRANSCENDENCE OF CREATION

Earlier we defined the word "transcendence" as:

• Existing apart from the material universe

Bible teacher and author Daniel Rhodes refers to the transcendence of God in his book, *The Logos of the Kingdom,* this way:

"God transcends all that we as humans see, hear, taste, smell or feel. God is Infinite in his being and nature and is therefore unlimited and unbound in all that He is and does. Since His realm of existence is infinitely beyond the finite limitations of spatial creation, our only proper response to Him is genuine reverence humility and obedience" (Rhodes. 2014 p 52).

Although we read the scriptures regarding the creation, we must rely on the Holy Spirit to reveal to us the reality of it all. Everything that is created throughout the universe originated in God. God stood outside of it and spoke to it and it appeared just as he declared it to be. Once you understand the logic of God and His intentions of how things are to be, you will understand the Kingdom of God and His righteousness.

"The essence of God's Kingdom is all about His Righteous Rule in His creation and in people. It's about how and why He Restores people to Himself and all that which was lost." (Rhodes, 2015. Direct quote).

There is nothing that has occurred anywhere throughout the universe that God did not foreknow. With that knowledge God has created the answer long before the problem was ever formed. Who, but Our Father, would, from the beginning, predestine us to be His children long before we set foot on the earth or passed the obstacle courses set before us? Who, but God, would consider placing seeds after its kind into everything he created therefore insuring multiplication, replenishment and fruitfulness of all he created.

Genesis 2:1 says,

"Thus the heavens and the earth were finished and all the host of them" (KJV).

The scripture shows God the Father, Jesus the Son and Holy Spirit moving in agreement according to the counsel of the Father's will.

Ephesians 1:11,

In Him also we have obtained an inheritance, being predestined according to the purpose of Him who work all thing according to the counsel of His will that we who first trusted in Christ should be to the praise of His glory (NKJV).

The scriptures show us that all of the creation was completed . . . finished along with all of the host of them in Genesis 2:1. This lets me know when God created the heavens in the earth that one time it was not all done in the Garden of Eden. It was done all over the earth. As a child, I was led to believe all of creation occurred in the Garden of Eden which always made me wonder when the Fall of Man occurred and Adam and Eve were driven from the Garden, where could they go. Now it is plain to see what God created in Genesis chapter 1 and finished in Genesis chapter 2 was all of creation and it was completed that one time. Never again did God have to stand out in space and create anything else. All of our past, present and future was started and completed in the beginning!

Therefore, after creation was completed Genesis 2: 8 occurred.

*And **the Lord God planted a garden** eastward in Eden; and there he put the man whom he had formed.*

It was then that verses 15-25 occurred.

15 And the Lord God took the man, and put him into the Garden of

Eden to dress it and to keep it. 16 And the Lord God commanded the man, saying, Of every tree of the garden thou mayest freely eat; 17 but of the tree of the knowledge of good and evil, thou shall not eat of it; for in the day that thou eatest thereof thou shalt surely die. 18 And the Lord God said, It is not good that the man should be alone; I will make him a help meet for him. 19 And out of the ground the Lord God formed every beast of the field, and every fowl of the air; and brought them unto Adam to see what he would call them; and whatsoever Adam called every living creature, that was the name thereof.

Vs 22 And the rib, which the Lord God had taken from man, made he a woman and brought her unto the man. 25 And they were both naked, and the man and his wife, and were not ashamed.

After the fall of man in Genesis chapter 3, we see when Adam and Eve were banished from the garden of Eden they were sent out into the world to cultivate the ground from which he had been made.

Genesis 3:23-24 declares,

So the Lord God banished them from the Garden of Eden, and he sent Adam out to cultivate the ground from which he had been made. 24 After sending them out, the Lord God stationed mighty cherubim to the east of the Garden of Eden. And he placed a flaming sword that flashed back and forth to guard the way to the tree of life (NIV).

After the fall, the bible says Adam and Eve were banished from the Garden. Banished to where? Outside the garden where all of the earth had also been completed, "in the beginning." We must remind ourselves, Father God is not man that when something happens he has to regroup. There is no White Out in his hip pocket, no eraser on his pencil and no "Oops" in His vocabulary. We are in a well-thought out, brilliantly-planned script of Our Omniscient God who knows exactly what He is doing and how to get us back to His original purpose in the Kingdom of God.

THE GENERATIONS OF CREATION

What I really appreciate is Genesis 2: 4 that declares the generations of the creation. Just as the genealogy of the offspring of man is declared throughout the Holy Word of God, so is the generation of the origination of creation.

*"These are the generations of the heavens and of the earth **when they were created,** in the day that the Lord God made the earth and the heavens, 5 **And every plant of the field before it was in the earth, and every herb of the field before it grew;** for the Lord God had not caused it to rain upon the earth and there was not a man to till the ground"* (KJV).

Did you get that? These are the generations of the heavens and the earth **when they were created.** Before rain had fallen on the earth and before man had a hand in cultivating the ground. It was all God. It all came forth out of what God said and the Word (Jesus) created it. Here is the answer to that age old question- What came first, the chicken or the egg? Hello **. . . Hello . . . according to the Word of God it was and is the chicken.** The sad part of this is man has the audacity to think he can do it better. Verse 4 of Genesis 2 states these are the generations of the heavens and the earth when they were created. In other words, these are the genealogies or origin of how creation came into being. According to the Merriam-Webster Dictionary:

Genealogy is 1: the history of a particular family showing how the different members of the family are related to each other 2: an account of the descent of a person, family, or group from an ancestor or from older forms 3: a regular descent of a person, family or group of organisms from a progenitor or older form: pedigree 4: an account of the origin and historical development of something.

In other words you can try to trace creation back as far as humanly possible only to discover the God who created it is **eternal** and has no point of origin because, He is **eternal.**

Moses, that mighty man of God, put it this way:

Lord, you have been our dwelling place in all generations. 2 Before the mountains were brought forth, or ever You had formed the earth and the world, Even from everlasting to everlasting, You are God. Psalms 90: 1-2. (New King James Version)."

God was so thorough in His creation that He stood outside of the universe, yet His voice walked in the Garden of Eden in the cool of the day! Look at God! Let's go deeper than that, God stands outside of time and space, yet speaks to us from eternity . . . and we hear his voice!!! Wow!

Go with me to Genesis 3:8-11,

8 And they (Adam and Eve) heard the voice of the Lord God walking, in the garden in the cool of the day; and Adam and his wife hid them-selves from the presence of the Lord God amongst the trees of the gar-den. 9 And the Lord God called unto Adam, and said unto him, "Where art thou?" 10 And he said, "I heard thy voice in the garden, and I was afraid, because I was naked; and I hid myself." 11 And he said, "Who told thee that thou wast naked? Hast thou eaten of the tree, whereof I commanded thee that thou shouldest not eat" (KJV)?

It all seemed so clear to me now. I have allowed the children to be taught a God who is creating one thing at a time as he goes along. Making it up as it appears necessary. How could I have missed this? The God I am preaching the adults is one as Isaiah 46: 10-11 states:

10 (God) Declaring the end from the beginning, and from ancient times the things that are not yet done, saying, My counsel shall stand, and I will do all my pleasure: 11 Calling a ravenous bird from the east, the man that executes my counsel from a far country: yea, I have spoken it, I will also bring it to pass; I have purposed it, I will also do it (KJV).

When we recognize the power of the spoken Word of God, we see all of creation is held together by the Word of Our Father through His Son Jesus. But let's think about this for a minute . . . exactly what all was God saying in those three word, "And God said?"

34

OH, THAT I MAY KNOW YOU

1 Corinthians 13:11-12 (KJV)

11 When I was a child, I spoke as a child, I understood as a child, I thought as a child; but when I became a man, I put away childish things. 12 For now we see through a glass, darkly; but then face to face; now I know in part; but then shall I know even as also I am known.

In Genesis chapter one, we see Our Father God steps out on nothing and creates everything. With our one dimensional glare through that darkened glass, we only comprehend what we see with our earth bound eyes or hear with our earth bound ears in the natural realm. We must adjust our thinking to that of the Great Father who has declared the end of all things from the beginning. As humans on the earth we are confined to time and space; therefore, what we do and what appears to us is within the confines of that limited area. Our Father God is not in time or space. As a matter of fact, He has created time and space; therefore, he moves freely about them as He wills. With this in mind we must expand our thinking to encompass that of our Creator. Remember, God is Spirit; therefore, when we deal with the things of God, we must be able to receive revelation from the Holy Spirit, who is our guide through the things of God. **First, please get this visual. In the beginning God created. God did not throw up or vomit out, He created.** The plan of God is organized and adaptive. With everything He created, there was a solution for every obstacle that may arise and an answer for every question that may be asked. He knew man would fall into sin, He knew he would have to send his Son Jesus to die for that sin and He knew you would be a part of this amazing plan. **Yes, we see both God's intentions for creation and ourselves in a dim mirror, but as we grow in maturity, we grow in clarity of who God is and who we are in Him. This is all part of God's Master Plan for us.** When did he know this . . . **in the begin-**

ning.

In Philippians 3:10 Paul says,

10 That I may know him (Jesus), and the power of his resurrection, and the fellowship of his sufferings, being made conformable unto his death; 11 If by any means I might attain unto the resurrection of the death (KJV).

In Exodus 33: 13 Moses says,

Now therefore, I pray thee, if I have found grace in thy sight, shew me now thy way that I may know thee, that I may find grace in thy sight; and consider that this nation is thy people (KJV).

How many times have you fallen on your knees and cried out to God, "Where are You . . . I want to know You?"

As a child, I would often ask people, "What does God look like, where is He when He is not talking to me? What does He like and what does He require of me?" I thought these were simple questions and worthy of answers, but everyone I spoke with would look at me strangely and say, "What curious questions for a child to ask." A family member once told me, "No one knows what God looks like or even what he is like, and hearing his voice is not a possibility." This disturbed me because, even as a child, I could sense him calling and drawing me. I could feel him close to me and when I spoke to him, I knew he heard every word. When sensing his Presence, each word was so full of power, potency, energy, strength and might, I found it impossible to explain to others what I perceived He had said. When I tried to relay to them what I was hearing and sensing, it would take me all day to try to explain what he had said in 30 seconds. Each word felt intentional and would come at the times I needed to hear them most. They were words specific to me . . . and to my situation. God was speaking to me and no one could make me think differently. He knew me. Now He wanted me to know and recognize Him. I was so inquisitive during those times, I would stop at nothing to get my questions answered. If man could not help me, I knew there had to be someone or something available to me that could.

My quest started with the Holy Bible (the written Word of the Living Word). When I first started learning about God there was only one biblical version available to me, and that was the King James Version. Although so much of it was difficult to understand, my mother took her time and explained as much of the Word as she could. As I continued to seek God through the pages of the Bible, I kept running across the mention of the Holy Spirit. I did not understand that in order to understand God and the work of Jesus, I needed to be introduced to the Holy Spirit. The bible was presenting Him as a person, but those around me explained "It" as an experience. I remember countless days as a ten year old tarrying at the altar for the "gift of speaking in tongues." I would go home disappointed wondering why my friend Jesus would leave me "hungering and thirsting" for the gift, but not receiving it. Many times I watched in amazement as those around me began to speak in their heavenly language, only to cry myself to sleep many nights wondering what was happening in my life hindering me from receiving such a great promise. Looking back now, I realize the entire search had been a set-up from God. The more I searched for Him, the more allusive He seemed to be; and the further away He seemed, the more I searched. Finally, years later, I was at home on my knees and told the Lord how I could not make it without evidence of His promise of the Holy Spirit in my life. I bared my soul to Him that day and before that prayer was finished, my mouth was overflowing with the glorious language of heaven. That night, alone on my knees, I was not only given a heavenly language, but the spiritual gifts were exploding within my spirit. I discovered who "God Is" through the discovery of the one God sent to teach and guide me; His Holy Spirit. Every day I learned more and more about the Father, Son and Holy

Spirit. It was all coming together and unfolding before me with such grace and understanding. After I was filled, I began to reflect on why it took me so long to receive from God. Could it be I was seeking the language just as I had seen others seeking, when in reality God wanted me to seek Him and with Him comes "everything I would ever need to become the prophet, teacher, visionary and pastor he was after from the beginning. **My vision for my life was one dimensional, but God sees so much further than we can ever know. God was after the very things He has placed within me from the beginning. I wanted the Holy Spirit to fill me so I could speak in tongues, but God was ready for me to be made aware of my destiny.** I saw Holy Spirit as 'tongues and a heavenly language' when in actuality He is so much more. He is the giver of spiritual gifts, our guide to the will of the Father, our comforter, teacher, revealer of truths and so much more. I was after 'tongues', but Holy Spirit was after me. Don't get discouraged if you don't receive what you see others receiving from God, you must consider who you are in God. The assignments we receive are given to us by the Holy Spirit as He wills. If you don't receive right away, it may be because your assignment requires more than you are aware of, so be diligent . . . and don't give up. God has already declared your end from the beginning. **Remember, He loves the chase because He knows you will love the end result when you see what he has in store for you. Trust Him.**

Proverbs 8:17 states,

I love them that love me; and those that seek me early shall find me (KJV).

Jeremiah 29:13 declares,

And ye shall seek me and find me, when ye shall search for me with all your heart (KJV).

I think Psalms 42:1-3 says it best,

1 As the hart pants and longs for the water brooks, so I pant and long for You, O God. 2 My inner self thirsts for God, for the living God.

When shall I come and behold the face of God? 3 My tears have been my food day and night, while men say to me all day long, Where is your God (ASV)?

I love this one, too, Psalms 63:1-2, 8

O God, thou art my God; early will I seek thee; my soul thirsteth for thee, my flesh longeth for thee in a dry and thirsty land, where no water is; 2 to see thy power and thy glory, so as I have seen thee in the sanctuary. 8 My soul followeth hard (close behind thee) after thee; thy right hand upholdeth me (KJV).

As God had **created** me in the beginning I could now sense and feel Him **forming** me into who He has declared me to be along my journey to my expected end. It was during this time I recognized the entire search for God was and is a set up by God. The Great I AM has an appointed time for us to seek for Him. The search starts as drops of water before a thirsty man or bread in the midst of famine. I believe there is an appointed time when God awakens us out of our drowsiness and presents Himself before us. He knows when we are ready, and He knows how to reach us at that appointed time. We must remember the draw from Our Father does not occur one time but at intervals throughout our walk with Him. Moses felt destiny while living in the palace of Pharaoh so he tried to deliver a slave using his own power. Like many of us, Moses could sense something needed to be done, but he did not know how to do it. He moved in his own strength and emotions not realizing it was not one slave that was attached to his assignment, but a massive, mighty people who had been in bondage for years and were now crying out to their God for deliverance. The zeal was there, but not the knowledge or revelation of the plan of God for the situation. The task before us has been set from the beginning in creation, but many times it is the forming of our character to meet that task that may slow the process.

CREATED THEN FORMED

Many times we try to understand God through the mind and thought processes of man. In our finite imaginations we think a thing is created when we see the finished work. The bible shows us, through the transcendence of Our Father God, creation begins in the beginning as a thought spoken and later formed into existence.

Look at what Paul says regarding Abraham in Romans 4: 17,

(As it is written, I have made thee a father of many nations,) before him whom he believed, even God, who quickeneth the dead, **and calleth those things which be not as though they were.** *18 Who against hope believed in hope, that he might become the father of many nations;* **according to that which was spoken, So shall thy seed be** (KJV).

After that creative thought is spoken, the forming begins. It is during the forming process we are made pliable to withstand the twist and turns that will occur during our becoming along our earthen journey.

Isaiah 43:7 says,

Even everyone that is called by my name: for I have created him for my glory, I have formed him: yea, I have made him (KJV).

But along with the forming of the Lord for our destiny comes the possibility of "shaping" that comes from the enemy for our destruction. Here is where choice comes into play. Proverbs 14: 12 puts it this way,

12 There is a way that seems right to a man, But its end is the way of death (NKJV).

In Genesis 1:26-27 God said,

And God said, Let us make man in our image, after our likeness; and let them have dominion over the fish of the sea, and over the fowl of

*the air, and over the cattle, and over all the earth, and over every creeping thing that creepeth upon the earth. 27 So **God created man** in his own image, in the image of God created he him; male and female created he them.*

Genesis 2:7 says,

*7 And the Lord **God formed man** of the dust of the ground and breathed into his nostrils the breath of life; and **man became a living soul.***

This verse lets us know God created us in his image. John 4: 24 says,

*24 **God is Spirit**; and they that worship Him must worship Him in spirit and in truth* (KJV).

God created man in his image and likeness and formed him from the dust of the ground, all in the beginning. When God created man and breathed into man's nostrils the breath of life man became a living soul. With that one breath from Our Father, man has been given the ability to become everything God has ordained him or her to be. In God's transcendence, He is able to create us in His image and form us into his likeness all at the same time. In other words, God started us and finished us with that one breath. It is with this one breath we can choose to praise or criticize, build up or tear down, bless or curse. You see, with that breath also comes the ability to make choices. We can choose to submit to the righteousness of our creator, or we can yield to the darkness that shapes us in iniquity and wickedness. All this is possible from that one breath from Our Father God given to man in the beginning.

King David said it this way in Psalms 51:1-6:

Have mercy upon me, O God, according to thy lovingkindness: according unto the multitude of they tender mercies blot out my transgressions. 2 Wash me thoroughly from mine iniquity and cleanse me

*from my sin. 3 For I acknowledge my transgressions; and my sin is ever before me. 4 Against thee, thee only, have I sinned, and done this evil in thy sight; that thou mightiest be justified when thou speakest, and be clear when thou judgest. 5 Behold, **I was shapen in iniquity;** and in sin did my mother conceive me. 6 Behold, thou desirest truth in the inward parts: and in the hidden part thou shalt make me to know wisdom* (KJV).

Do you see that? David said, "I was shapen in iniquity." The Word of God says he was formed in the image and likeness of God, yet through the course of David's journey in life he found he could be shaped into wickedness. This is why we must allow the spirit man within us to be born again. If you are a born again believer, it is this spirit man living inside you that maintains your connection to God and allows you to communicate with the Holy Spirit and He with you.

It is this **formed man** that we read about in Genesis 2:7-8, 21. This formed man was placed in the Garden of Eden and it is from this formed man's rib, woman was taken.

*7 And the Lord formed man of the dust of the ground and breathed into his nostrils the breath of life; and man became a living soul. 8 And the Lord God planted a garden eastward in Eden; and there he put the man whom he had **formed*** (KJV).

21 And the Lord God caused a deep sleep to fall upon Adam, and he slept: and he took one of his ribs, and closed up the flesh instead thereof; 22 And the rib, which the Lord had taken from man, made he a woman, and brought her unto the man (KJV).

In was in this forming when God placed man on the earth and equipped him with an earth suit capable of adapting to the atmosphere of the earth. That earth suit is our flesh. The flesh is formed from the dust of the ground and is aware of the visible, tangible things on the earth.

Romans 8:12-14

Therefore, brethren, we are debtors, not to the flesh, to live after the flesh. 13 For if ye live after the flesh, ye shall die; but if ye through the Spirit do mortify the deeds of the body, ye shall live (KJV).

Romans 7:18

For I know that in me (that is, in my flesh,) dwelleth no good thing; for to will is present with me; but how to perform that which is good I find not (KJV).

Romans 8: 8

So then they that are in the flesh cannot please God (KJV).

The soul of the man is his mind where his thoughts and emotions are processed. It is that "living soul" that has to come unto the subjection of the Holy Spirit or will of God. Our soul is made up of our emotions, intellect, consciousness and will. Our soul enables us to experience thoughts, and emotions and allows us to figure things out based on the most influential force surrounding us. If not renewed, through the Word of God, the soul of man can easily be led by carnal persuasions.

Romans 8: 7 says,

Because the carnal mind is enmity against God: for it is not subject to the law of God, neither indeed can be (KJV).

Romans 12:1-2

I beseech you therefore, brethren, by the mercies of God, that ye present your bodies a living sacrifice, holy, acceptable unto God, which is your reasonable service. 2 And be not conformed to this world; but be ye transformed by the renewing of your mind, that ye may prove, what is that good, and acceptable, and perfect, will of God (KJV).

It is the man created (spirit man) in the image of God (who is Spirit) who is capable of maintaining and sustaining communications with God. It is through our spirit man of the heart we can communicate with God who is Spirit through his gift of the Holy Spirit.

Romans 8:

14 For as many as are led by the Spirit of God, they are the sons of God (KJV).

Proverbs 20:27

The spirit of man is the candle of the Lord, searching all the inward parts of the belly (KJV).

The Holy Spirit cannot communicate with our earth suit (flesh) or our minds (souls) which caters to and concentrates on the things of the world. That is why the bible states in

Romans 8:5-8,

5 For they that are after the flesh do mind the things of the flesh; but they that are after the Spirit the things of the Spirit. 6 For to be carnally minded is death; but to be spiritually minded is life and peace. 7 Because the carnal mind is enmity against God; for it is not subject to the law of God, neither indeed can be. 8 So then they that are in the flesh cannot please God (KJV).

Now we see in the beginning God created man in his own image and likeness. But even in heaven there was an insurrection where Lucifer tried to confront God in God's Spiritual Kingdom. In his pride, Lucifer with a third of the angels in heaven confronted the Father, Son and Holy Spirit who are One. During this battle, God cast Lucifer out of Heaven along with a third of the angels who were influenced by this rebellion.

Isaiah 14:12-14

12 How art thou fallen from heaven, O Lucifer son of the morning! How art thou cut down to the ground which didst weaken the nations! 13 For thou hast said in thine heart, I will ascend into heaven I will exalt my throne above the stars of God; I will sit also upon the mount of the congregation, in the sides of the north; 14 I will ascend above the heights of the clouds; I will be like the most High (KJV).

The bible tells us Lucifer (now called Satan) and his angels (now demons) were cast from heaven as lightening and thrown to earth.

Isaiah 14:15

Yet thou shalt be brought down to hell, to the sides of the pit. 16 They that see thee shall narrowly look upon thee, and consider thee, saying, Is this the man that made the earth to tremble, that did shake kingdoms; 17 That made the world as a wilderness, and destroyed the cities thereof; that opened not the house of his prisoners? 18 All the kings of the nations even all of them, lie in glory, everyone in his own house. 19 But thou art cast out of thy grave like an abominable branch, and as the raiment of those that are slain, thrust through with a sword, that go down to the stones of the pit; as a carcass trodden under feet (KJV).

Luke 10:18,

And he (Jesus) said unto them, I beheld Satan as lightning fall from heaven (KJV).

Now we see how Satan was defeated in the Spirit realm by Our Triune God, but now must be defeated in the earth realm by the Power of God in our regenerated (spirit) now formed and placed in an earth suit (flesh) and dealing with a renewed mind (soul). Our Father has given His children all the tools and power necessary to, not only fight this battle, but win the war. The weapons of our warfare are not carnal, but mighty through God to the pulling down of strong holds.

No strong hold can resist the weapons given to us by our Father God. Our strongest weapon is the ability and authority to use the Mighty Name of Jesus Our Savior, who died on the cross, shed His blood and rose from the dead with all power in His hand!

1 Thessalonians 5: 23,

And the very God of peace sanctify you wholly; and I pray God your whole spirit and soul and body be preserved blameless unto the coming of our Lord Jesus Christ (KJV).

Remember, God is not making this up as we go along, this is His Master Plan put in place from the beginning. In the beginning God knew we needed one to go before us on the earth in order to accomplish this feat. One would have thought it to be the first man Adam, but as we see in the book of Genesis he was not able to withstand the temptation of the evil one (Satan). Therefore God's plan included a man not only with the Spirit of God, but born of a woman (formed in flesh, born of the water) and the ability to resist the enemy by making righteous choices (soul) by the leading of (Holy Spirit). This man is Jesus the Christ who was born not only the Son of God but the Son of man (yet without sin).

Hebrews 4:15,

For we have not an high priest which cannot be touched with the feeling of our infirmities; but was in all points tempted like as we are, yet without sin (KJV).

1 Corinthians 15:45,

And it is written, The first Adam was made a living soul; the last Adam was made a quickening spirit. 46 Howbeit that was not first which is spiritual, but that which is natural; and afterward that which is spiritual. 47 The first man is of the earth, earthy; the second man is the Lord from heaven (KJV).

It is through Jesus's birth, death, burial and resurrection that we are now able to take dominion of the earth and all that God created. We do this through our regenerated spirits which allow us to stand in the position of sons of God. But this can only take place after the new birth (regeneration of the spirit man) and the renewing of our mind (taking on the mind of Christ).

John 3:3,

Jesus answered and said unto him, Verily, verily, I say unto thee, Except a man be born again, he cannot see the kingdom of God (KJV).

Jesus told Nicodemus, "Ye must be born again."

Romans 10: 9-10,

That if thou shalt confess with thy mouth the Lord Jesus and shalt believe in thine heart that God hath raised him from the dead, thou shalt be saved. 10 For with the heart man believeth unto righteousness; and with the mouth confession is made unto salvation (KJV).

John 17: 14,

14 I have given them thy word; and the world hath hated them because they are not of the world even as I am not of the world. 15 I pray not that thou shouldest take them out of the world, but that thou shouldest keep them from the evil. 16 They are not of the world even as I am not of the world. 17 Sanctify them through thy truth; thy word is truth (KJV).

When was all of this established . . . in the beginning.

JESUS, THE WORD

One of the hardest things for me in writing this book is to stay within the confines of the man-made definitions to describe what Our Triune God accomplished during His creations. So much more happened during these time than we will ever know because we continue to see through a glass darkly on a one dimensional level. **With everything "God said", Jesus the Word created, but not in the sense many of us can comprehend. Remember the Word of God teaches us that God's thoughts are higher than our thoughts, so when Jesus was creating the words spoken by the Father, Life was being ignited into every created fiber of every created being. Just as God said it, Jesus the Word created it and Life filled it.**

Look at Genesis 1:27-28 with me again and notice while man was being created, purpose, life and direction were being infused into him all at the same time.

27 So God created man in his own image, in the image of God created he him; male and female created he them. 28 And God blessed them, and God said unto them, Be fruitful, and multiply, and replenish the earth and subdue it: and have dominion over the fish of the sea, and over the fowl of the air, and over every living thing that moveth upon the earth (KJV).

Now, in the next verses you will notice God assures man that everything he has spoken to Him by the Word is available to him. Everything God expects from what He has created can be accomplished.

Continue with Genesis 1:29-31,

29 And God said, Behold, I have given you every herb bearing seed, which is upon the face of all the earth, and every tree, in the which is the fruit of a tree yielding seed; to you it shall be for meat. 30 And to every beast of the earth, and to every fowl of the air, and to everything that creepeth upon the earth, wherein there is life, I have given every green herb for meat: and it was so. 31 And God saw every thing that he had made, and behold, it was very good. And the evening and the morning were the sixth day (KJV).

Now we see in Genesis 1:27 and Genesis 2:7 how God created and formed man outside the Garden of Eden and afterwards placed him in the Garden of Eden.

7 And the Lord God formed man of the dust of the ground and breathed into his nostrils the breath of life; and man became a living soul. 8 And the Lord God planted a garden eastward in Eden; and there he put the man whom he had formed. (KJV)

Here we see life outside the Garden was filled with God. Everything created was created by God. Everything spoken was spoken by Our Great Triune God. After God breathed into man the breath of life we see the becoming of man into a living soul. God did not create us as robots to do his bidding. He created us with the ability to choose just as he did the Angels in heaven. But even in an atmosphere where God has His Righteous Rule, as in Heaven, choice can cause disruption and chaos. But God, in His infinite wisdom, considered all of this "in the beginning" and provides a way of escape for His people. It is in this wisdom of God that He places the man he has formed into an environment of peace, love, provision, life, knowledge and, yes, even evil.

*9 And out of the ground made the Lord God to grow every tree that is pleasant to the sight, and good for food; the tree of life also in the midst of the garden, **and the tree of knowledge of good and evil.** Genesis 2:9 (KJV)*

We must remember the evil is not there to tempt us for God

cannot be tempted by evil, but evil is allowed in the garden to activate the discerning tools of engagement created within us as we become what God has created us to be.

James 1:12-15,

Blessed is the man that endures temptation; for when he has been approved, he will receive the crown of life which the Lord has promised to those who love Him. **13 Let no one say when he is tempted, "I am tempted by God", for God cannot be tempted by evil, nor does He Himself tempt anyone.** *14 But each one is tempted when he is drawn away by his own desires and enticed. 15 Then, when desire has conceived, it gives birth to sin; and sin, when it is full-grown, brings forth death* (NKJV).

What I hear the Lord saying to us is anyone can live a Godly life when they are in a controlled environment of love, joy, peace and harmony. But it is not until we are confronted with evil, chaos, conflict and the various unfavorable choices of life that we find out who we really are. The Fruit of the Spirit (Galatians 5) are not bought in a store or passed out at a fruit stand, but are grown out of our human spirit as we learn to trust and depend on Our Father God in every area of our lives. God does not want us loving Him out of obligation; but by choice. Choice based on who He is, not what He does for us. God already know what we are capable of because He created us and we are His idea. He needs for us to know we are not just conquerors over disruptions in our life and atmosphere, but more than conquerors over the seen and unseen, natural and supernatural through Jesus Our Lord and Savior. Our choice must be an individualized decision based on our walk and knowledge of God. What better way to know Him than to choose to have Him at our sides as we walk through this journey of **becoming** what God has already said?

Throughout the book of Isaiah you will see the concept of creating and forming. Isaiah 45:7 says,

I form the light, and create darkness: I make peace, and create evil: I the Lord do all these things (KJV).

Isaiah 43:7 says,

Even everyone that is called by my name: for I have created him for my glory, I have formed him: yea, I have made him (KJV).

THE CREATING OF JACOB AND FORMING OF ISRAEL

But now thus saith the Lord that created thee, O Jacob and he that formed thee O Israel, Fear not: for I have redeemed thee, I have called thee by thy name; thou art mine. Isaiah 43:1 (KJV)

The word **Genesis** according to Webster's New World College Dictionary (ed. 4) is defined as:

- The way in which something comes to be;

- Beginning

- Origin

I often find myself reading the genealogies in the bible because they depict the beginning of families and their origins. They, also, share the physical ending of one family and the beginning of another. In Genesis 12:1 we see how God calls Abram to come out from his family and from everything he thinks he knows about himself and step out into where God is and discover who God has declared him to be.

Now the Lord had said unto Abram, Get thee out of thy country, and from thy kindred, and from thy father's house, unto a land that I will shew thee (KJV) .

In order for Abraham to become the *father of many nations*, whom God had ordained and declared him to be, he had to be willing to begin again. God's word to Abram was to leave; leave everything you know to be and begin again with what I have said. This is the beginning of faith for Abram because everything God requires of him will not materialize until he begins his journey from the seen into the unseen, from the tangible to the unknown. The Lord calls Abram (who had no children because his wife Sarai was barren) the *father of many nations*. To many of us this seems strange, but in the eyes and mind of

God, it was already so for God declared Abram's end from the beginning. 2 Corinthians 4:18 states,

18 While we look not at the things which are seen, but at the things which are not seen: for the things which are seen are temporal; but the thing which are not seen are eternal (KJV).

It took many years for Abram, the son of Terah, to become Abraham, the *father of many nations.* As outsiders looking in, it may seem Abram made mistakes along his faith journey. What we must remember is every move we make has already been seen by God long before He chose us and changed our names. What we see as failures, God sees as opportunities to teach us how to depend on Him more.

Abraham's journey produced two sons; Ishmael who was born of his wife's maid servant, Hagar, and Isaac who was born of Abraham's wife, Sarah. Ishmael was known as the child of the flesh and Isaac as the child of promise. What Abraham did not understand in the beginning, was for him to become the *father of many nations* would involve more life adjustments than those of just himself and Sarah. Attached to your destiny are more people than you can ever imagine. You may be called to start the work, but others may be ordained to take it to its completion; therefore we must be careful whom we choose to bless or curse or give up on. You may be cursing or giving up on your successor.

Isaac was Abraham's son and successor. Although the title of *father of many nations* was bestowed upon Abraham, the conclusion of the matter would involve his descendants. Isaac, the son of Abraham, marries Rebekah when he is 40 years old. After Isaac prayed for her to conceive, Rebekah became pregnant with twin boys. Throughout her pregnancy it was as if the children struggled against each other in her womb, therefore, Rebekah sought the Lord for an answer to her distress. Genesis 25: 23 is God's reply to Rebekah regarding the struggling children in her womb,

The Lord said to her [The founders of] two nations are in your womb, and the separation of two peoples has begun in your body; the one people shall be stronger than the other, and the elder shall serve the younger (AMP).

We see from the beginning the twins struggle because of their destinies. They are two nations and one has been ordained to be stronger than the other and the older of the two will serve the younger. This was declared by God in the beginning. As you read this text you will discover the younger son is Jacob and the older twin is Esau. Keep in mind no matter what it looks like in the natural, God has already declared the end from the beginning.

Genesis 25: 27-28,

When the boys grew up, Esau was a cunning and skilled hunter, a man of the outdoors; but Jacob was a plain and quiet man, dwelling in tents. 28 And Isaac loved [and was partial to] Esau, because he ate of Esau's game; but Rebekah loved Jacob (AMP).

Throughout their childhoods you will notice neither boy seemed to be without struggles or challenges, but Jacob appeared to be more level headed and logical in his decision making considering future consequences which may incur, while Esau concentrated on the here and now with little thought of consequences. Jacob, although declared to be the stronger of the two, appears weaker in his outer appearance and is described as a quiet boy, content with living in tent. Esau, prophesied to be the weaker twin, displayed physically strength and was obviously more agile than his brother. The Bible states Esau was busy developing his skills of hunting and exploring the great outdoors and such abilities caught the admiration and affections of his father Isaac. In light of these differences, each parent had a favorite son for the scripture states,

And Isaac loved [and was partial to] Esau, because he ate of Esau's game; but Rebekah loved Jacob.

Although each parent may have felt justified in their reasoning of partiality toward the twins, it is this kind of behavior that can easily shape ones personality and self-esteem. Jacob and Esau were twins yet they were treated differently by their parents. Could it be Isaac loved Esau best because he considered him the firstborn son, for during this time the firstborn held a position of honor and pride in the family bloodline? Someone as agile as Esau would be useful in battle and in defending the home front from intruders as well as maintaining the needs of the family.

What about Rebekah, could it be she was partial to Jacob because she was the one the Lord spoke to regarding his destiny and believed it was up to her to make it come to pass? Let's look closer into this situation for a moment.

In Genesis 25:23 we read how Rebekah received word that the elder son (Esau) would serve the younger (Jacob) and that one people would be stronger than the other. But the scripture does not let us know if she shared this information with her husband Isaac. Perhaps Rebekah translated strength to be wisdom and foresight instead of the obvious brawn and manly physique which was admired and expected during these times.

What we do see in the scripture is how Esau despised his birthright enough to sell it to his younger brother for a bowl of stew, simply, because he was hungry and thirsty. Esau was willing to sell his God given spiritual strength in a natural moment of weakness.

Genesis 25:29-34,

Now Jacob cooked a stew; and Esau came in from the field, and he was weary. 30 And Esau said to Jacob, "Please feed me with that same

red stew, for I am weary." Therefore his name was called Edom. 31
But Jacob said, "Sell me your birthright as of this day." 32 And Esau
said, "Look, I am about to die; so what is this birthright to me." 33
Then Jacob said, "Swear to me as of this day." So he swore to him,
and sold his birthright to Jacob. 34 And Jacob gave Esau bread and
stew of lentils; then he ate and drank, arose, and went his way. Thus
Esau despised his birthright (NKJV).

The bible does not tell us Jacob stole the birthright, but simply that
he seized the moment to obtain it from his brother Esau. We see how
Jacob's father Isaac loved Esau. Could Jacob have possibly considered
that in obtaining the birthright this would win his father's love and acceptance? It is easy to see how Jacob could have a problem with feeling invisible to his father even after buying the birthright from Esau.
Would his father Isaac even recognize such a transaction? Would or
could this cause Isaac to see Jacob in a better light? Would Jacob now
have to fear his brother Esau because of what had transpired? So many
questions! Remember we are talking about the **forming of Jacob**. Remember when God spoke to Rebekah He was speaking into the life of
Jacob and Esau. But once the twins were born it may have appeared to
Jacob that his mother made a mistake or misinterpreted what God was
saying. Instead of Jacob's life being one of blessings he found himself
without a voice (quiet man) and living a simple life (in tents) while his
brother Esau was loved of his father and able to satisfy Isaac's appetite
with his venison. Can you relate to Jacob? Has anyone ever spoken a
word over you that you were highly favored of God, only to have your
life turned upside down waiting for that word to come to pass? And
what about what happened when the boys were older and their father
Isaac's eye grew dim? Let us read Genesis 27:1-10,

Now it came to pass, when Isaac was old and his eyes were so dim that
he could not see, that he called Esau his older son and said to him,
"My son." And he answered him, "Here I am." 2 Then he said, "Be-

hold now, I am old. I do not know the day of my death. 3 Now therefore please take your weapons, your quiver and your bow, and go out to the field and hunt game for me. 4 And make me savory food such as I love, and bring it to me that I may eat that my soul may bless you before I die." 5 Now Rebekah was listening when Isaac spoke to Esau his son. And Esau went to the field to hunt game and to bring it. 6 So Rebekah spoke to Jacob her son, saying, "Indeed I heard your father speak to Esau your brother, saying, 7 'Bring me game and make savory food for me, that I may eat it and bless you in the presence of the Lord before my death.' 8 Now therefore, my son, obey my voice according to what I command you. 9 Go now to the flock and bring me from there two choice kids of the goats, and I will make savory food from them for your father, such as he loves. 10 Then you shall take it to your father, which he may eat it, and that he may bless you before his death" (NKJV).

Throughout Jacob's life we have seen his desire to win the respect and love of his father, but here his mother Rebekah is showing him a way to manipulate and trick his father into speaking the first born blessing over him instead of his brother Esau. What must Jacob have been thinking at this point? Could his mother think the only way his father will bless him is if he thinks he is his brother Esau? If his father does bless him will it really be him (Jacob) that is being blessed or Esau, in his father's eyes. Does this mean his father does not consider him good enough for a blessing although he has obtained the birthright from his brother? How is this situation affecting how Jacob sees and feels about himself? Let's continue,

11 And Jacob said to Rebekah his mother, "Look, Esau my brother is a hairy man, and I am a smooth-skinned man. 12 Perhaps my father will feel me, and I shall seem to be a deceiver to him; and I shall bring a curse on myself and not a blessing." 13 But his mother said to him, "let your curse be on me, my son; only obey my voice, and go, get them for me." 14 And he went and got them and brought them to his mother, and his mother made savory food, such as his father loved. 15 Then Rebekah took the choice clothes of her son Esau, which were with her in the house and put them on Jacob her younger son. 16 And she put the skins of the kids of the goats on his hands and on the smooth part of his neck. 17 Then she gave the savory food and the bread which she had prepared, into the hand of her son Jacob.

18 So he went to his father and said, "My father." And he said, "Here I am. **Who are you, my son?" 19 Jacob said to his father, "I am Esau your firstborn;** I have done just as you told me; please arise, sit and eat of my game, **that your soul may bless me**" (NKJV).

Oh how this must have made Jacob feel. He is longing for recognition and a sign of acceptance from his father, but in order to receive it he believes he has to be someone else. He does not understand the blessing has already been declared over him (during creation) and it will come to pass not based on what is done here, but based on what was done in the beginning.

20 But Isaac said to his son, "How is it that you have found it so quickly, my son?" And he said, "Because the Lord your God brought it to me." 21 Isaac said to Jacob, "Please come near, that I may feel you, my son, whether you are really my son Esau or not." **22 So Jacob went near to Isaac his father, and he felt him and said, "The voice is Jacob's voice, but the hands are the hands of Esau." 23 And he did not recognize him because his hands were hairy like his brother Esau's hands; so he blessed him.** 24 Then he said, **"Are you really my son Esau?" He said, "I am."** 25 He said, "Bring it near to me, and I will eat of my son's game, so that my soul may bless you." So he brought it near to him, and he ate: and he brought him wine, and he drank. 26 Then his father Isaac said to him, "Come near now and kiss me, my son." And he came near and kissed him; and he smelled the smell of his clothing and blessed him . . ." (NKJV).

From that moment, the life of Jacob is one filled with manipulation and deceit either on his part or that of someone trying to control him. Jacob also has favorable things happen in his life, perhaps in his mind, stemming from a blessing given him by his father in the name of his brother Esau. Can you imagine the questions that must have filled his heart such as, "how far can I go on a stolen blessing?" "Will I ever be free to live a blessed life as Jacob?" These are questions that can only be answered by the God of creation. Jacob's steps had been ordered of God although the means by which many things may have been done were not ordained of God. God is the one who called and chose Jacob and He already had a plan in place to allay all of Jacobs's fears and concerns and the end result will be a change in attitude, personality, perception of God and a name change. A name that will speak to who he really is.

Let look at Genesis 32:22-31. By this time, Jacob has left home and started a family. Many thing has transpired over the years. Jacob has two wives, two female servants and eleven children, but still has not made peace with his brother Esau.

22 And he arose that night and took his two wives, his two female servants, and his eleven sons and crossed over the ford of Jabbok. 23 He took them, sent them over the brook, and sent over what he had. 24 **Then Jacob was left alone***; and a Man wrestled with him until the breaking of day. 25 Now when He saw that He did not prevail against him, He touched the socket of his hip; and the socket of Jacob's hip was out of joint as He wrestled with him. 26 And He said, "Let Me go, for the day breaks."* **But he said, "I will not let You go unless You bless me!"**

27 **So He said to him, "What is your name?" He said, "Jacob"** **(NKJV).**

Jacob is now married with children and still dealing with the same identity crisis. Now he has an Angel of the Lord standing before him and all he can think about is **"Will you Bless Me . . . My name is Jacob. Can you speak over Me?"** Jacob is asking to be blessed as himself. He wants to know God is doing these things for him because of who he is, not based on a lie or deception of another.

*28 And He said, **"Your name shall no longer be called Jacob, but Israel**; for you have struggled with **God and with men,** and have prevailed." 29 **Then Jacob asked, saying, "Tell me Your name, I pray." And He said, "Why is it that you ask about My name?" And He blessed him there.** 30 So Jacob called the name of the place Peniel; "**For I have seen God face to face** and my life is preserved"* (NKJV).

Did you get that? God is letting Jacob know He has seen his struggle with man (his brother, his parent, his father in law) and you have even struggled with God and prevailed. Now you are more than Jacob, you are who I have declared you to be from the beginning, you are Israel. From that moment, Jacob no longer had to depend on the words others had spoken over him, he now has received his own word from the Lord. Jacob has heard from God himself and received the blessing from the mouth of his God face to face spoken in the beginning.

OUR MULTI-DIMENSIONAL GOD

As we take a look at the many dimensions in God, please note Father God, Jesus and the Holy Spirit are One God. Jesus is everything the Father is. Jesus speaks not of Himself but what He hears the Father speak that is what He does.

John 12:49,

For I have not spoken of myself; but the Father which sent me, he gave me a commandment, what I should say, and what I should speak. (KJV)

Jesus is the King of the Kingdom of God. He is not becoming . . . He already was, is and is to come for He is the same yesterday, today and forever. Jesus is our Lord and Savior sent by the Father to die for the sins of man and show us how to return the Righteous Rule of the Father back to the earth. Jesus is our way to salvation.

John 3:16

For God so loved the world, that he gave his only begotten Son, that whosoever believeth in him should not perish, but have everlasting life (KJV).

Jesus is the creator of all that is. He is the Lamb of God and Our High Priest making intercessions for us to the Father God. Jesus is the Eternal Word of God.

John 1:1 says,

In the beginning was the Word, and the Word was with God, and the Word was God. He was in the beginning with God. All things were made through Him and without Him nothing was made that was made (NKJV).

He is the Word made flesh that dwelt among us.

John 1:14 says,

And the Word became flesh and dwelt among us, and we beheld His glory, the glory as of the only begotten of the Father, full of grace and truth (NKJV).

Jesus is our perfect example. Jesus is the Alpha and Omega, the beginning and the end, the first and the last.

Revelations 1:8,

I am Alpha and Omega, the beginning and the ending, saith the Lord, which was and which is to come, the Almighty (KJV).

Jesus is our brother and friend. He is the way, the truth and the Life. Jesus is the Light of the world.

John 9:5 states,

As long as I am in the world, I am the light of the world (KJV).

John 15:13

Greater love hath no man than this, that a man lay down his life for his friends (KJV).

We are heirs and joint heirs with Jesus in the Kingdom of God.

Romans 8:16-17,

The Spirit itself beareth witness with our spirit, that we are the children of God: 17 And if children, then heirs; heirs of God, and joint heirs with Christ: if so be that we suffer with him, that we may be also glorified together (KJV).

Everything Our Father God is, Jesus is. Jesus is the Son of God.

Hebrews 4:14 says of Jesus,

Seeing then that we have a great High Priest who has passed through the heavens, Jesus the Son of God, let us hold fast our confession. 15 For we do not have a High Priest who cannot sympathize with our weaknesses, but was in all points tempted as we are, yet without sin. 16 Let us therefore come boldly to the throne of grace that we may obtain mercy and find grace to help in time of need (NKJV).

Jesus is the Christ.

Matthew 16:16,

And Simon Peter answered and said, Thou art the Christ, the Son of the living God (KJV).

John 6:69,

And we believe and are sure that thou art that Christ, the Son of the Living God (KJV).

When Jesus walked the earth, He was the Son of God yet many times referred to himself as the Son of man for our benefit.

Luke 22: 67-71,

Art thou the Christ? Tell us. And he said unto them, If I tell you, ye will not believe: 68 And if I also ask you ye will not answer me, nor let me go. 69 Hereafter shall the Son of man sit on the right hand of the power of God. 70 Then said they all, Art thou then the Son of God? And he said unto them, Ye say that I am. 71 And they said, What need we any further witness? For we ourselves have heard of his own mouth (KJV).

Jesus is our perfect example. He showed us how to exist in the natural realm as sons of man but access the spiritual realm as sons of God.

1 John 3:1-2,

Behold, what manner of love the Father hath bestowed upon us, that

63

we should be called the sons of God: therefore the world knoweth us not, because it knew him not. 2 Beloved, now are we the sons of God, and it doth not yet appear what we shall be: but we know that, when he shall appear, we shall be like him; for we shall see him as he is (KJV).

As sons of man, we are aware of the things of the earth that are seen, felt, heard and spoken on the earth, through our natural, earth-bound senses. As sons of God, we are aware of the invisible things in nature, in the heavens, and in the spirit realms i.e. angelic and demonic forces. These things in the spirit realm are seen through the eyes of the Spirit and faith in God. In this duel role, we can cast out devils, heal the sick, speak with new tongues, be led by the Spirit of God and set the captives free.

John 3:5

Jesus answered, Verily, verily, I say unto thee, Except a man be born of water and of the Spirit, he cannot enter into the kingdom of God (KJV).

Throughout the bible Jesus is referred to as the Son of God and the Son of man (born of the water (natural birth) and of the Spirit. All of these things were declared in the beginning.

Mark 16:17-18

17 And these signs shall follow them that believe; In my name shall they cast out devils; they shall speak with new tongues; 18 They shall take up serpents; and if they drink any deadly thing, it shall not hurt them; they shall lay hands on the sick and they shall recover (KJV).

Luke 9:52-56 speaks of Jesus in this passage,

And sent messengers before his face; and they went, and entered into a village of the Samaritans, to make ready for him. 53 And they did not receive him, because his face was as though he would go to Jerusalem. 54 And when his disciples James and John saw this, they said, Lord, wilt thou that we command fire to come down from heaven, and consume them, even as Elias did? 55 But he turned, and rebuked them, and said, Ye know not what manner of spirit ye are of. 56 For the Son of man is not come to destroy men's lives, but to save them. And they went to another village (KJV).

Yes, Jesus dwelt with us as the Son of man, but He is the Son of God. As Son of man, Jesus dwelt among us, teaching, preaching and showing us how to love unconditionally and forgive our enemies; but as the Son of God, He did so much more. Jesus walked on water, walked through crowds that were trying to kill him, healed the sick, raised the dead, spoke to the elements, was transfigured before his disciples and commanded demons to bow. **It was in His humanity He taught us and in His divinity He showed us the way.** Then He promised, because we belong to the Father, what He did, we would do on the earth and even greater things.

St John 14:12,

Verily, verily, I say unto you, He that believeth on me, the works that I do shall he do also; and greater works than these shall he do; because I go unto my Father (KJV).

Through my relationship with Jesus, I have come to believe this is the greatest miracle of all. Jesus allowed us to see his humanity full on, but when it comes to his divinity He allows us to see only shadows. Remember everything God is, Jesus is. Jesus could have shown his transcendence at any time, but because of his love for the Father and the Father's love for us along with His desire to please the Father, Jesus submitted Himself to the will of what the Father had declared. Thank you, Jesus!!!!!

We see ourselves in duo roles in the Kingdom of God and we oft times see our God in the same light. **But God is Multi-Dimensional.** There are so many layers and characteristics of God that in our finite minds we cannot fathom them all. Can you imagine it. Our Father is the God of all the universe and we are His children. We belong to Him. Wow! This same God (Our Father) **wants** to have a close relationship with us. We are His children, heirs and joint heirs with Jesus Our Lord. It is during our deepened relationship with Father God we get to see some of the sides of Him. We are not only privy to His presence, but we have a front row seat as we get to experience His acts and His ways. To know Him is to know how to please Him, just as Jesus does. We need to find out what God wants out of this relationship. What does He want us to know about Him? Let's discuss what the bible tells us about Our Father God.

First Our God is Transcendent: I have already given definitions for this characteristic of God, now let's give its scriptural foundation:

Let's start with Job 11: 7-10,

Can you find out the deep things of God, or can you by searching find out the limits of the Almighty [explore His depths, ascend to His heights, extend to His breadths, and comprehend His infinite perfection]? 8 His wisdom is as high as the heights of heaven! What can you do? It is deeper than Sheol (the place of the dead)! What can you know? 9 Longer in measure [and scope] is it than the earth, and broader than the sea. 10 If [God] sweeps in and arrests and calls into judgement, who can hinder Him? [If He is against a man, who shall call Him to account for it?] (AMP).

In other words, who knows enough to argue with God? Our thinking and rationale is nowhere close to His. Remember, He is the justifier, not us. Look how Isaiah puts it in chapter 55: 8-9,

8 For My thoughts are not your thoughts, neither are your ways My

ways, says the Lord. 9 For as the heavens are higher than the earth, so are My ways higher than your ways and My thoughts than your thoughts (AMP).

Exodus 34: 6-8 says,

And the Lord passed by before him, and proclaimed, The Lord! The Lord! A God merciful and gracious, slow to anger, and abundant in loving-kindness and truth, 7 Keeping mercy and loving-kindness for thousands forgiving iniquity and transgression and sin, but Who will by no means clear the guilty visiting the iniquity of the fathers upon the children and the children's children, to the third and fourth generations. 8 And Moses made haste to bow his head toward the earth and worship (AMP).

In God's infinite wisdom, He could have created each of us to be robots for which He could download His wisdom and instructions into us. It could have been so easy, but instead, Our Father created us in His image and likeness, giving us choice and will. In His infinite wisdom, He had already given choice to the Angelic beings in Heaven and Lucifer, with a third of the angels, rebelled against God's righteous rule causing insurrection to occur. Yet, with this in mind, God still believes in us enough to send His only begotten Son Jesus to die for our sins. As high as the heavens are from the earth and the east is from the west, the Love of God transcends it all.

Paul says it this way in Romans 8:38-39,

For I am persuaded beyond doubt (am sure) that neither death nor life, nor angels nor principalities, nor things impending and threatening nor things to come, nor powers, 39 Nor height nor depth, nor anything else in all creation will be able to separate us from the love of God which is in Christ Jesus our Lord (AMP).

Our God is Omniscient. Merriam-Webster Dictionary defines omniscient as:

- Knowing everything: having unlimited understanding or knowledge

- Having infinite awareness; understanding, and insight

- Possessed of universal or complete knowledge

There are no surprises with God. He knows all things and their outcomes.

In the gospel of Luke 14: 28-30 Jesus states,

For which of you, intending to build a tower, sitteth not down first, and counteth the cost, whether he have sufficient to finish it? 29 Lest haply, after he hath laid the foundation, and is not able to finish it, all that behold it begin to mock him, 30 Saying, This man began to build, and was not able to finish. 31 Or what king, going to make war against another king, sitteth not down first and consulteth whether he be able with ten thousand to meet him that cometh against him with twenty thousand? 32 Or else, while the other is yet a great way off, he sendeth an ambassage, and desireth conditions of peace. 33 So likewise, whosoever he be of you that forsaketh not all that he hath, he cannot be my disciple (KJV).

Our Father knew and considered every possibilities before he created one single thing. The heavens, earth and all that lives therein has been fearfully and wonderfully made and considered. All of creation was and is an original thought in the Heart of God. He established the way of escape long before the captivity was declared. He placed the answers here long before the questions were formed. He knows the outcome long before the battle begins. Throughout the Bible, are example after example of how God speaks the end of the situation long before anyone knows there is a situation about to begin. The story of Gideon in the sixth chapter of Judges is a perfect example. Let's examine it.

The NIV reads thus, Judges 1:1-6,

The Israelites did evil in the Lord's sight. So the Lord handed them over to the Midianites for seven years. 2 The Midianites were so cruel that the Israelites made hiding places for themselves in the mountains, caves, and strongholds. 3 Whenever the Israelites planted their crops, marauders from Midian, Amalek, and the people of the east would attack Israel, 4 camping in the land and destroying crops as far away as Gaza. They left the Israelites with nothing to eat, taking all the sheep, goats, cattle, and donkeys. 5 These enemy hordes, coming with their livestock and tents, were as thick as locusts; they arrived on droves of camels too numerous to count. And they stayed until the land was stripped bare. 6 So Israel was reduced to starvation by the Midianites. **Then the Israelites cried out to the Lord for help.**

Did you get that? Long before the Israelites cried out, God was aware the situation was coming. He knew how difficult it would get for His people, and He already had an answer waiting in the wings. Although the Israelites had disobeyed God and began to serve the gods of the enemy, He still had a plan to deliver them. As we continue to read this story, we will discover that the answer was a disillusioned young man by the name of Gideon.

Judges 6:11 (NIV)

11 Then the angel of the Lord came and sat beneath the great tree at Ophrah, which belonged to Joash of the clan of Abiezer. Gideon son of Joash was threshing wheat at the bottom of a winepress to hide the grain from the Midianites. 12 The angel of the Lord appeared to him and said, **"Mighty hero, the Lord is with you!"**

13 "Sir", Gideon replied, "if the Lord is with us why has all this happened to us? And where are all the miracles our ancestors told us about? Didn't they say, "The Lord brought us up out of Egypt"? But now the Lord has abandoned us and handed us over to the Midianites."

14 Then the Lord turned to him and said, **"Go with the strength you have, and rescue Israel from the Midianites. I am sending you!"**

15 "But Lord," Gideon replied, "how can I rescue Israel? My clan is the weakest in the whole tribe of Manasseh and I am the least in my entire family!"

16 The Lord said to him, **"I will be with you. And you will destroy the Midianites as if you were fighting against one man."**

Are you getting this? When did God declare Israel's victory . . . in the beginning. When did God declare Gideon would be the one to lead them to that victory . . . in the beginning. In the book of Genesis when God said, "Let there be," He was not just speaking to that time and space. He was speaking into the earth and to His people of the earth - past, present and future! God does not see things as we see them. He sees beyond what is seen and hears beyond what is heard and speaks into the atmosphere and declares what He will. Remember, we are not an afterthought . . . we are a fore thought. In the beginning God created and said! Visualize Our Almighty Father standing before the universe seeing our past, present and future all in one glance. He sees it all at the same time!

Our God is Eternal. Merriam-Webster Dictionary defines eternal as:

- Having no beginning and no end in time; lasting forever

- Existing at all times; always true or valid

- Seeming to last forever

As we discussed earlier, God does not live in time and space; we do. Long before God created the heavens and the earth, the origin or idea of it was already in Him. He has all eternity to determine what He wants because what he desire is who He is. Job chapter 23 verse 13-14 puts it this way,

But he is in one mind, and who can turn him? And what his soul desireth, even that he doeth (KJV).

And what about what is said about Jesus the creator of all God said,

Revelations 1:8

I am Alpha and Omega, the beginning and the ending, saith the Lord, which is, and which was, and which is to come, the Almighty. (KJV)

The screen before Our Father God shows our past, present and future. There is nothing hidden from Him because He is the originator of all things. All things originate in him and ends in him, yet he has no beginning or ending. He has created our time and space capsule but also the ability for us to live outside that capsule with Him for eternity. When He said, "Let there be . . ." he was speaking to our past, present and future all at the same time.

Job 24: 1

Why, seeing times are not hidden from the Almighty, do they that know him not see his days? (KJV).

Remember what Revelations 4:8 declares about Him,

8 And the four beast had each of them six wings about him; and they were full of eyes within; and they rest not day and night, saying, Holy, holy, holy, Lord God Almighty, which was, and is, and is to come (KJV).

Our God is Sovereign. Merriam-Webster defines sovereign as:

- Having unlimited power or authority; superlative in quality

- Not limited; supreme

- Having independent authority and the right to govern itself

- Having undisputed as ascendancy

The Bible in Ecclesiastes 5: 1-2, reminds us how we are to present ourselves in the presence of the Lord.

Walk prudently when you go to the house of God; and draw near to hear rather than to give the sacrifice of fools for they do not know that they do evil. 2 Do not be rash with your mouth, and let not your heart utter anything hastily before God. For God is in heaven, and you on earth; Therefore let your words be few (NKJV).

Sovereignty speaks of independent authority as in Hebrews 6: 13:

For when God made promise to Abraham because he could swear by no greater, he sware by himself (KJV).

God does not need anyone's permission to do anything. He does not ask advice, but He does His own good pleasure. Job 23:13 says,

But he is in one mind and who can turn him? And what his soul desireth, even that he doeth (KJV).

In other words, God has already made up his mind about you. He knows what he has placed in you, and his expectation of you is great! So stop saying what you can't do or that this is too hard to do. God knows differently. From the beginning, He declared your end and what His soul desireth, that shall he do. There is no famine or lack in God. He is the God who not only placed within you enough of everything to get the job done, but **More than Enough**. So go on and throw up, pull a temper tantrum and fall out in the floor; it will not do any good.

He has already made up his mind - you are a mighty warrior and more than a conqueror through Christ Jesus. So in other words, "Get over yourself, and grow up." You can do this!!!!!!!!!!

God is timeless, yet timely. We live on the earth in a time-space continuum, but our Father God lives in eternity. Therefore, God has determined a time and season for all things pertaining to His people. There are appointed times for us set up by the Father who does all things well. Our job is to keep the appointment and pass the test. Let's take another look at Job 23: 14.

For He (God) performeth the thing that is appointed for me; and many such things are with him (KJV).

Ecclesiastes 3: 1-8 states,

To every thing there is a season and a time to every purpose under the heavens; 2 A time to be born, and a time to die; a time to plant, and a time to pluck up that which is planted; 3 A time to kill, and a time to heal; a time to break down, and a time to build up; 4 A time to weep and a time to laugh; a time to mourn, and a time to dance; 5 A time to cast away stones, and a time to gather stones together; a time to embrace, and a time to refrain from embracing; 6 A time to get, and a time to lose; a time to keep, and a time to cast away; 7 A time to rend, and a time to sew; a time to keep silence, and a time to speak; 8 A time to love, and a time to hate; a time of war and a time of peace (KJV).

I know things may seem chaotic at times, but we must remember we are on God's time table, not our own. Because of His love for us, He has not only allowed things to come our way but has placed every-thing we need in that time and space to overcome and live through the moment. We are never meant to die in the battle, but to overcome. Remember, God breathed into our nostrils, His breath of life. He has armed us with every advantage possible. He also armed us with these special promises,

Isaiah 43:2-3a,

When thou passest through the waters, I will be with thee; and through the rivers, they shall not overflow thee: when thou walkest through the fire, thou shalt not be burned; neither shall the flame kindle upon thee. 3(a) For I am the Lord thy God, the Holy One of Israel, thy Savior: (KJV).

Hebrews 13:5,

Let your conversation be without covetousness; and be content with such things as ye have: for he hath said, I will never leave thee, not forsake thee. (KJV)

Job 14:14 states,

If a man die, shall he live again, all the days of my appointed time will I wait, till my change come. (KJV)

If you have doubt about appointed times in God, look at the heavens, animals and the elements. They are all aware of the times with and in God. Look at Jeremiah 8:7,

Yea, the stork in the heaven knoweth her appointed times; and the turtle and the crane and the swallow observe the time of their coming; but my people know not the judgement of the Lord. (KJV)

Just like our Father God has appointed days for us to fulfill His will and purpose for us, the plans He has for us have an appointed time to manifest.

Jeremiah 29:11-13 (NIV)

*For I know the plans I have for you, says the Lord. "They are plans for good and not for disaster, to give you a future and a hope. 12 **In those***

days when you pray, *I will listen. 13 If you look for me wholehearted-ly, you will find me.*

Here is the same verse in the KJV,

For I know the thoughts that I think toward you, saith the Lord, thoughts of peace and not of evil, to give you an expected end. 12 ***Then shall ye call upon me, and ye shall go and pray unto me,*** *and I will hearken unto you.*

Every plan the Father puts in place has a time table for which it will be the most effective. Read Habakkuk 2:1-3

I will stand upon my watch, and set me upon the tower, and will watch to see what he will say unto me, and what I shall answer when I am reproved. 2 And the Lord answered me and said, Write the vision, and make it plain upon tables, that he may run that readeth it. 3 ***For the vision is yet for an appointed time but at the end it shall speak and not lie; though it tarry wait for it;*** *because it will surely come, it will not tarry* (KJV).

I love this scripture! The prophet lets us know that even if it does not happen right away, wait for it. Why? Because God has declared it will come to pass. We can't base our faith on things we see or suppose. We can't give in to our emotions. If Our God said it, He will bring it to pass. Our faith must have its bases in Our Father God and in the finished work of Jesus Our Lord. Remember who said it – Our Father God. Remember when He said it . . . **in the beginning.**

Our God is self-existent. Webster's New World College Dictionary (ed. 4) defines self-existent as:

• Existing of or by itself without external cause or agency

John 5:26 says,

For as the Father hath life in himself; so hath he given to the Son to have life in himself; (KJV)

In the AMP it says,

26 For even as the Father has life in Himself and is self-existent, so He has given to the Son to have life in Himself and be self-existent.

In other words, there is no external power source for God. He is the power source. Everything lead to Him. He is the Great "I AM", the beginning and the ending, the first and the last, the alpha and omega. He has the first and last say. He does not ask anyone or anything for advice.

The Book of Hebrews puts it this way in chapter 6 verse 13,

For when God made promise to Abraham, because he could swear by no greater, he swear by himself (KJV).

Our God is self-revealing. Webster's New World College Dictionary (ed. 4) defines self-revealing as:

- Revealing or expressing one's inner most thoughts, emotions, etc.

Isaiah 53:1

Who hath believed our report? And to whom is the arm of the Lord revealed? (KJV)

We are the children of God and He wants us to know Him. To know Him is to love Him. He does not want us to be afraid to approach Him, but to come boldly unto Him knowing He is for us. God also loves the chase. He loves for us to seek Him with all of our heart, not because we want something from Him, but simply because He is Our Father.

Jeremiah 29: 13 says,

And ye shall seek me, and find me, when ye shall search for me with all of your heart. 14 And I will be found of you, saith the Lord; and I will turn away your captivity, and I will gather you from all the nations, and from all the places whither I have driven you, saith the Lord; and I will bring you again into the place whence I caused you to be carried away captive.

Did you hear that? There are times when Our Father allows things to happen or come into our lives just to provide an opportunity for us to seek Him, cry out to Him, and allow Him to rescue us. Read Jeremiah 29:13 again remembering God could have prevented their captivity, but He allowed it to come to pass because many times we think it's by our own abilities we escape or make things better. In actuality, if it had not been for the Lord who is on our side, we would have been destroyed and swallowed up. God wants to be our rescuer, but He also wants us to get the revelation that He knows what He is doing.

Psalms 124: 1-3

If it had not been the Lord who was on our side, now may Israel say; 2 If it had not been the Lord who was on our side, when men rose up against us: 3 Then they had swallowed us up quick, when their wrath was kindled against us; (KJV).

1 Chronicles 28:9b

. . . for the Lord searches all hearts, and understandeth all the imagi-nations of the thoughts; if thou seek him, he will be found of thee, but if thou forsake him, he will cast thee off forever (KJV).

Matthew 11:25-27

*At that time Jesus answered and said, I thank thee, O Father, Lord of heaven and earth, because thou hast hid these things from the wise and prudent, and hast revealed them unto babes. 26 Even so, Father; for so it seemed good in thy sight. **27 All things are delivered unto me of my Father; and no man knoweth the Son, but the Father; neither knoweth any man the Father, save the son, and he to whomsoever the Son will reveal him*** (KJV).

God is revealing: Webster's New World College Dictionary (ed. 4) defines revealing as:

- To draw back the veil

- To make known something hidden or kept secret

- To make known by supernatural or divine means

So far, we have established how Our Father God knows all things and is not limited in his understanding of anything or anyone.

John 6:44

No one is able to come to Me unless the Father who sent Me attracts and draws him and gives him the desire to come to me, and [then] I will raise him up [from the dead] in the last day (AMP).

Jesus says in John 15: 16,

*Ye have not chosen me, but I have chosen you, and ordained you, that ye should go and bring forth fruit, and that your fruit should remain; that whatsoever ye shall ask of the Father in my name, **He may give it you*** (KJV).

When looking at these scriptures, we must understand this is God speaking through Jesus and the Holy Spirit, for they are all One. Jesus says in John 14:10, "**The words that I speak unto you I speak not of myself, but the Father that dwelleth in me, he doeth the work**", and according to John 16:13 the Holy Spirit does not speak of Himself but whatsoever he shall hear of the Father.

John 16:13

*Howbeit when he, the Spirit of truth, is come, he will guide you into all truth; for he shall not speak of himself; **but whatsoever he shall hear, that shall he speak; and he will shew you things to come*** (KJV).

As God reveals Himself to us, he reveals truth. Our God is the God of Truth. Jesus declares in John 17:17

Sanctify them through thy truth; thy word is truth (KJV).

In John 8:32 Jesus says,

And ye shall know the truth, and the truth shall make you free (KJV) .

And of Himself Jesus say in John 14:6,

Jesus saith unto him, I am the way, the truth, and the life; no man cometh unto the Father but by me (KJV).

Since the fall of man in the Garden of Eden, man has had to wade through lies, deceit and false perceptions conjured up from the prince of the air, Satan himself. Without the leading of the Holy Spirit, we would fall prey to every lie, deception, spiritual wickedness in high places, evil accusations, demonic wiles, Satanic traps, seducing spirits and doctrine of devils. This is why Our Father has made a way escape by allowing us to enter into His presence and come into the knowledge of truth through His Word. Long ago, man had to rely on the priest and prophets to speak to God for them, but because of the finished work of Jesus Our Savior, we can boldly go to the throne of God ourselves. It is in His presence we find fullness of joy and get to know Him for ourselves. Our Father longs to reveal Himself to His children.

Luke 12:2

Nothing is [so closely] covered up that it will not be revealed, or hidden that it will not be known (AMP).

Once Our Father God has revealed Himself to us through Jesus and the guidance of the Holy Spirit, we will no longer be impressed with the wisdom of man. As sons of God we will embrace the wisdom of the Father and know that we are part of a divine plan set in motion by the Great Triune God and know it is He who is in charge and does all things well.

1 Corinthians 2:4-10

4 And my speech and my preaching was not with enticing words of man's wisdom, but in demonstration of the Spirit and of power; 5 That your faith should not stand in the wisdom of men, but in the power of God. 6 Howbeit we speak wisdom among them that are perfect; yet not the wisdom of this world, nor of the princes of this world, that come to nought: ***7 But we speak the wisdom of God in a mystery, even the hidden wisdom, which God ordained before the world unto our glory;*** *8 Which none of the princes of this world knew; for had they known it, they would not have crucified the Lord of glory. 9 But as it is written, Eye hath not seen, nor ear heard, neither have entered into the heart of man, the things which God hath prepared for them that love him.* ***10 But God hath revealed them unto us by his Spirit: for the Spirit searcheth all things, yea, the deep things of God*** (KJV).

WHAT THE SEARCH WILL REVEAL

Before I answer this question, I need to make it clear no one knows the "Why's" of God. He is God and does what He pleases when and how He pleases. But I am beginning to recognize why some of the things that have happened in my life have transpired the way they have. Let's look at Jeremiah 1:5-8 in the Message Bible,

"Before I shaped you in the womb, I knew all about you. Before you saw the light of day, I had holy plans for you: A prophet to the nations—that's what I had in mind for you." 6 But I said, "Hold it, Master God! Look at me. I don't know anything. I'm only a boy!"7-8 God told me, "Don't say, 'I'm only a boy.' I'll tell you where to go and you'll go there. I'll tell you what to say and you'll say it. Don't be afraid of a soul. I'll be right there, looking after you."

Father God knows everything there is to know about me. He knows me better than I know myself. When He speaks to me he speaks to my end from the beginning, not from my present position. Because He knows all of these things, He knows what it will take to keep me on track and on time. I have appointments I need to keep with destiny. I can't afford to be late or too early. That's why I must be led by the Holy Spirit in all I say and do. Paul tells the church at Corinth, *"the manifestation of the Spirit is given to every man to **profit withal."*** (1 Corinthians 12:7).

 He also says in verse 11 that, *"all these (gifts of the Spirit) worketh that one and the selfsame Spirit, **dividing to every man severally as he will.** "* (KJV).

 The assignment set before each of us is too important to be left up to us to make it work. Our Father has already spoken what has to happen and has called and chosen us to carry it out just like He has declared it. Therefore, God knows my personality, temperament, strengths, and weaknesses and how to utilize them for the task ahead. When we are in school or college, we take test to discover what type of "learners" we are and what works best for us in order for us to do the best job possible. From these test, the instructors develop the curriculum around our strengths and weaknesses, making sure to concentrate on the things we may not have considered along the way. In order for us to know how well we are doing, we are given periodic exams or quizzes. Every test and exam has purpose and is prepared to allow the student to reach his or her potential and goals. If an earthly instructor can devise a plan such as this, how much more Our Almighty Omniscient Father God. We must remember God sees our past, present and future all at the same time. He knows when we are on course or when we are headed for ship wreck. We see through a glass darkly and only in part, therefore, we must be led of the Holy Spirit in order to please the Father and allow His will to be done on earth as it is in Heaven. Holy Spirit is a gift from Our Father to help us navigate through the pits, snares, wiles and strategies of the evil one, but He also is there to teach us how to know the voice and will of the Father as we become sons of God.

The more we know about God, the more we learn to trust Him. The more time we spend in His presence the more we learn to yield our will to the will of the Father. Our thoughts and souls must become one with Christ. We must take on the mind of Christ. Jesus is the Head of the church and we are His body. Remember, a body with two heads is a monster. It is not your way and God's way; it is God's way, alone.

Every gift God has placed within us has been given from the beginning. As we come into the knowledge of the Will of God for us those gifts are stirred up and manifested as the Spirit wills. Although I had experienced the gifts of the Spirit in my life as a child, it wasn't until I became a minister of the gospel that I had my first vision. I did not know it was still possible to have visions. I had read about visions in the Bible, but I had never met anyone who had actually experienced one. Could this be one of the reasons God kept my husband and me isolated from other ministries and denominations during that time of church infancy? The answer to that questions is an emphatic, yes!!! We cannot base our walk on the walk of others. God knew I had a tendency to take at face value what others would tell me regarding what God used to do versus what He will do today. I thought visions were for those in the Old Testament or for the apostle only, but because I didn't know better, when the Spirit of God appeared to me in visions, I received the experience and the message without reservation or hesitancy. Now, we must understand, Holy Spirit does not minister to everyone the same way. The experience with Him is based on your assignment, your creative make up and as the Spirit wills. As a matter of fact, I have learned the majority of God's people have never received visions of any kind. Many of us receive revelation from reading the word of God and while in prayer. It is also important to know not all visions or manifestations are from God. Therefore, we are not to desire visions or pray for them. Remember the Holy Spirit gives gifts as He wills. We must allow the Holy Spirit to minister to us the things of God and not try to manipulate our way into an experience, this can be spiritually detrimental.

The gifts of the Holy Spirit must also come with wisdom and truth. Regarding visions, not all visions are the result of an encounter with God. Many appear as a result of late night eating or snacks or ones over active imagination. Others may appear as distractions sent from demonic influences. Because of these possibilities, it is important not to seek or pray for such revelations or manifestation because they can easily lead you down paths of destructions. The Word of God does not tell us to be led by the revelations or visions but to be "led by the Holy Spirit." Like Moses and the burning bush, God knows how to get the attention of each of us based on the kind of "learner" we are. I am a visual learner; therefore, much of how the Spirit ministers to me is visual. I have learned with each manifestation of the Spirit it is important not to interpret the experience using your own understanding.

With each revelation of the Spirit of Truth comes the divine purpose and plan of God along with the timing for that plan to manifest in the earth. Visions and revelations do not come to present you as some great wonder, but they come to prepare the people of God for the next move of God.

Daniel 2:19

Then was the secret revealed unto Daniel in a night vision. Then Daniel blessed the God of heaven (KJV).

THE VISION OF THE WHIRLWIND

One Friday evening I was invited to attend a revival service with a dear friend. The evangelist that evening was one whom I have grown to love and respect and one who is truly anointed of God. During these revivals the gifts of the Holy Spirit are evident and the people are moved, healed, touched and delivered by the power of God. This night was no exception. When I attend her revivals, I like to serve in any way possible, so I was awaiting her instructions regarding what she wanted me to do. As instructed, throughout the evening, I assisted the ushers in catching those slain in the Spirit, praying for the sick and instructing those in need of salvation. In the midst of this powerful move of God, I felt the presence of His Holy Spirit come upon me in a mighty way. Because I have been given many vision by the Lord, I did not want to become a distraction in the service; therefore I found myself receding to the back of the church into a corner in order to see or hear what the Lord would say to me. While standing there:

I saw a whirlwind start up in the middle of the sanctuary. It started small and grew large enough to encompass the sanctuary and the congregation within itself. Before long, it grew large enough to include the outer structures of the building and begin to swallow up the city. Although the perception before me was that of a whirlwind, the presence controlling the wind was intimate and personalized. I knew without a doubt who I was looking at . . . He was so familiar. Although I had never seen Him before . . . I knew His presence. . . I knew Him. It was the intimate presence of the Holy Spirit of God. I could not see His face or his form but I knew Him therefore, I was not afraid. I opened my mouth to speak, but I could not. Yet, I heard myself say to Him, "I know you."

He answered me and said, "Look into the wind." As I stared into the whirlwind I saw multiple sets of eyes throughout its makeup. The eyes were big, small, expressive, kind, fiery, gentle, forgiving, loving and fierce all at the same time. This scene overwhelmed me but also comforted me in the same breath. Before I could utter a word, I heard Him say, "Listen." As I listened, I heard voices . . . where were they coming from? I began to look at the congregation and I noticed their lips were not moving, but I could hear what they were thinking. I heard some thinking about what they were going to do when they got home, others were asking God to help them to be healed and delivered tonight during the revival.

I heard one man say, "This is a charade, none of this is real," while another woman was praying for deliverance for her baby, whom she had left in the care of someone else while she attended the service. I heard the voices of some discussing their lifestyles, others hoping their secrets would not be revealed, while others were rehearsing their day and plotting and planning their tomorrow. After listening for a while, I begin to question how God could allow the people to be that disconnected and aloof when all God wanted to do was to help them.

Before I could speak this, I heard Holy Spirit say, "The same way I tolerated your secrets and thoughts." Because of the awesomeness of the moment, I had failed to realize just as I was hearing their thoughts and secrets, my Lord was also aware of mine.

"Oh Lord, please forgive me," I cried. All of a sudden, I noticed the voices were becoming louder and multidirectional. They were the voices of the city, of mothers and fathers, the homeless and the lost. Finally, I said, "Holy Spirit, I hear their voices, their secrets, their thoughts. What are you telling me?"

Then He asked me a question I will remember the rest of my life:

"Can you know their thoughts and not judge them . . .

Can you know their secrets and still minister to them?"

Thinking this was to be an addition to the gifts He had already stirred within me, I opened my mouth to say, "Yes, Lord, I can" . . . but instead, I heard myself say, "Lord, only you know."

Slowly, as the vision began to dissipate, I found myself on the floor in the corner of the church. When I came to myself, I was uttering these words, "Lord, fix me so I can handle this; help me become what you need me to be."

As soon as the service was over, I rushed to the car and sat in silence, not knowing what to do with what I had experienced. When I got home, I awakened my husband and shared with him what had happened. Tear flowed down my face as I tried to relate to him every moment of the encounter with Holy Spirit. "What do I do with this . . .?" I asked. "I have no idea where to put this in my life. I have no point of reference for what Holy Spirit has spoken to me."

Then I heard my husband say, "Terry, the same Father who has given this to you will make it clear and give you peace."

He was so right because less than three weeks later, while waiting for a class at the University of Memphis, I felt that same Presence come over me. Sitting alone in the lobby of the music department, I begin to hear the thoughts of the people around me. I could hear their secrets, anxieties, discouragements, joys and fears. Instead of judging them based on their outward appearances I was compelled to pray for them as though they were my own children. I no longer saw them as strangers but as the called and chosen trying to find their way to God. I prayed for God to give them peace and time to recognize who they are in Him. I began to remember life at their age before I knew God. Their thoughts were once my thoughts, their situations were once my own. I begin to relate to their loneliness, failures and feelings of insecurities and pressure. The Holy Spirit had given me the power to relate to this group of young adults and the wisdom to intercede for them on a more intimate level. It was only when I recognized my instructor calling my name that I realized once again I had drifted into the realm of the spirit where time and space does not exist and one is allowed to see and hear what the Father allows. It was such a humbling experience. As I gathered my books and class work to follow my instructor to her office, I heard myself whisper to God, "please, help me become whatever it is you are in need of. Teach me, Holy Spirit."

You may ask yourself why God gives a vision such as this to his people. "What is He saying to us?" People of God, unless you have been living under a rock or had your head buried in the sand, you are aware of the deception that continues to grip the people of the earth. We have generations of families who no longer go to church and will blatantly say, "There is no God." None of this is surprising to God, for the Bible declares,

Ecclesiastes 6:1-2,

There is an evil which I have seen under the sun, and it lies heavily upon men: 2 A man to whom God has given riches, possessions, and honor, so that he lacks nothing for his soul of all that he might desire, yet God does not give him the power or capacity to enjoy them [things which are gifts from God], but a stranger [in whom he has no interest succeeds him and] consumes and enjoys them. This is vanity (emptiness, falsity, and futility); it is a sore affliction! [Luke 12:20.] (AMP).

There is nothing new under the sun. Atheistic beliefs fill the air waves, social media, television prime time shows, children's programming, day cares, public education and the political arenas. Children's cartoons express the importance of recognizing a person can be a "mule and a duck" in the same body and be acceptable to God and society. We see just because the building has a sign that says "Church of God" on the outside does not mean it is of Christian persuasion or that they are worshiping Our Heavenly Father God on the inside. We can join the rank of those who whine and scoff wondering, "What are we going to do?" or we can join the Body of Believers in the fray for the souls of the people for whom Jesus gave His life. There is a reason we are here in this specific time and space. There is a reason we are reading this book here and now. You could have been born any time, why now? You are here now because of the all the questions we have discussed. The questions are ringing in the ears of the people because, in the beginning, God sent you to be the **answer**. We are not as those who have no hope. God in His infinite wisdom sent us to the earth for such a time as this. The blood of Jesus is just as potent now as ever, and the message of the cross and resurrection of Our Lord is clear. In order for us to reach this people, here and now, we must yield to the potter's wheel and become what Our Father God has declared us to be. This is not a job for the part-time Bible-thumper. The only ones who will stand when this dust settles are the sons of God. The Apostle Paul puts it this way in Romans 8:18-23,

[But what of that?] For I consider that the sufferings of this present time (this present life) are not worth being compared with the glory that is about to be revealed to us and in us and for us and conferred on us! 19 For [even the whole] creation (all nature) waits expectantly and longs earnestly for God's sons to be made known [waits for the revealing, the disclosing of their son ship]. 20 For the creation (nature) was subjected to frailty (to futility, condemned to frustration), not because of some intentional fault on its part, but by the will of Him Who so subjected it-[yet] with the hope [Eccl. 1:2.] 21 That nature (creation) itself will be set free from its bondage to decay and corruption [and gain an entrance] into the glorious freedom of God's children. 22 We know that the whole creation [of irrational creatures] has been moaning together in the pains of labor until now. [Jer. 12:4, 11.] 23 And not only the creation, but we ourselves too, who have and enjoy the first fruits of the [Holy] Spirit [a foretaste of the blissful things to come] groan inwardly as we wait for the redemption of our bodies [from sensuality and the grave, which will reveal] our adoption (our manifestation as God's sons) (AMP).

AGREEING WITH WHAT GOD SAID

Do two walk together except they make an appointment and have agreed? Amos 3:3 (AMP)

In the beginning God created the heaven and the earth. In doing so He was of one mind. In Genesis Chapter One, we can see how God said it, Jesus created it and the Holy Spirit moved upon the face of it. The Father, Son and Holy Spirit work as one to create and implement. Throughout the gospels in the New Testament, we see Jesus reminding the disciples, "When you see me you see the Father."

John 14:8-10

Philip said unto Him, "Lord show us the Father and it is sufficient for us. 9 Jesus said unto him, "Have I been with you so long, and yet you have not known Me, Philip? He who has seen Me has seen the Father; so how can you say, 'Show us the Father'? 10 Do you not believe that I am in the Father, and the Father in Me? The words that I speak to you I do not speak on My own authority; but the Father who dwells in Me does the works (NKJV).

The Father, Son and Holy Spirit are one, therefore agree as one. The Father is of one mind therefore, there is only one script and that script precedes out of the Mouth of the Father. Jesus and the Holy Spirit know the mind of the Father, so all they have to do is just learn their lines. Jesus says, "I speak not of myself but what the Father speaks." Jesus says of the Holy Spirit, "He will not speak of Himself but what he hears the Father say, that will He speak."

John 16:13

However, when He, the Spirit of truth, has come He will guide you into all truth; for He will not speak on His own authority but whatever He hears He will speak; and He will tell you things to come (NKJV).

90

Jesus also says of Himself in John 12:49-50

For I have not spoken on My own authority; but the Father who sent Me gave Me a command, what I should say and what I should speak. 50 And I know that His command is everlasting life. Therefore, whatever I speak, just as the Father has told Me, so I speak (NKJV).

Wow, can it get any plainer than that? How can we be manifested as sons of God when we are not willing to yield ourselves to the Father who has the one and only master plan? When God stepped out onto nothing and spoke the Word, Jesus had to create everything the Father spoke, according to the Father's specificity. Jesus knows the Mind of God and what He requires because He is One with the Father. They are not the same in mind only, but according to John 16: 14-16, Jesus says to the disciples, when the Holy Spirit comes upon you He is going to spend His time telling you about me and showing you the things that are mine because what is mine belongs to the Father, therefore, will belong to you when you become one with me.

John 16:14-16

He will glorify Me, for He will take of what is Mine and declare it to you. 15 All things that the Father has are Mine. Therefore I said that He will take of Mine and declare it to you. 16 "A little while, and you will not see Me; and again a little while, and you will see Me, because I go to the Father" (NKJV).

I believe many times we stress out because we are so busy trying to navigate our way through this life. We can't find our way because we don't have the plan. We will never be able to make things work depending on our own understanding and man-made wisdom. Proverbs 16:25 says it this way,

There is a way that seems right to a man, But its end is the way of death (NKJV).

There is only one way that leads to eternal life. That way is Jesus.

John 14:6 says,

Jesus said to him, "I am the way, the truth, and the life. No one comes to the Father except through me (NKJV).

In John chapter 17 Jesus spends His time praying to the Father that we be made one with Him. We say when we die we will have eternal life, but do we really know what eternal life is? Look at John 17:1-6:

*Jesus spoke these words, lifted up His eyes to heaven, and said: "Father, the hour has come, Glorify Your Son, that Your Son also may glorify You, 2 as You have given Him authority over all flesh that He should give eternal life to as many as You have given Him. 3 **And this is eternal life, that they may know You, the only true God, and Jesus Christ whom You have sent**. 4 I have glorified You on the earth. I have finished the work which You have given Me to do. 5 And now, O Father, glorify Me together with Yourself, with the glory which I had with You before the world was. 6 "I have manifested Your name to the men whom You have given Me out of the world. They were Yours, You gave them to Me, and they have kept Your word . . ."* (NKJV).

For us to accomplish what we must in this end time, we must know the mind and heart of the Father. We must be one with the Lord Jesus who is our Savior, King of the Kingdom of God and our perfect example. Jesus' prayer to the Father in John 17: 11 is that we might be one as He and the Father are one. Ephesians 4:3 talks about the unity of the Spirit in the bond of peace. This lets us know the Holy Spirit has given us everything needed to help us walk and work as one. Ephesians 4:11-13 says,

And he gave some, apostles; and some, prophets; and some, evangelists; and some, pastors and teachers; 12 for the perfecting of the saints for the work of the ministry, for the edifying of the body of

Christ; 13 Till we all come in the unity of the faith, and of the knowl-edge of the Son of God unto a perfect man, unto the measure of the stature of the fullness of Christ; (KJV).

In other words, wherever we are in our Christian walk, the Holy Spirit has placed within our grasp the necessary ministry gifts needed to smooth out our rough edges and point us to Jesus. We are without excuse because each of these ministry positions are sent to the body of Christ to help mature us that we be no longer babes toss about by every unholy doctrine and belief. According to 1 Corinthians 15:58 we are to be:

Therefore, my beloved brethren, be steadfast, immovable, always abounding in the work of the Lord, knowing that your labor is not in vain in the Lord (NKJV).

Our Father's Master Plan calls for the use of men and women who are called, ordained by God and chosen to walk in the offices of the apostles, prophets, evangelists, pastors and teachers. He is not going to send angels from heaven to do this work, but He has already put in place a body of believers led by the Holy Spirit who He has declared to be the ears, eyes, voice and ambassadors for this mighty restoration of His Righteous Rule on the earth. In order to do this God's way, we must be one with the Father as we walk in the unity of the faith, and of the knowledge of the Son of God unto a mature man. We must be in agreement with Our Triune God.

WALKING IN AGREEMENT WITH GOD

The Story of Jesus and Martha

In John chapter 11 we find the story frequently referred to as that of "The Raising of Lazarus from the Dead." I like to think of this text as the *Covenant of Jesus and Martha* where "deep calls unto deep." Let me show you why. Remember in the beginning, **"God said".** The lives of Mary, Martha and Lazarus were created and spoken into "in the beginning" of time. God already knew what had to happen in this family and the outcome. This family was and still is part of God's grand plan. God is the originator of all things. Jesus declares in John 12:49-50:

For I have not spoken of myself; but the Father which sent me, he gave me a commandment, what I should say and that I should speak. 50 And I know that his commandment is life everlasting: whatsoever I speak therefore, even as the Father said unto me, so I speak. (KJV)

Remember Jesus was in the beginning with God, therefore when Jesus came to the earth in human form He was the Son of God, but he also called Himself the Son of man. Jesus had a divine appointment with Lazarus and his sisters. He was aware of it because of His connection with the Father, but Mary, Martha and Lazarus were like we are "seeing through a glass darkly." As we go through these scriptures keep in mind how Jesus is the author and finisher of our faith (Hebrews 12:2). During this time, part of the Father's master plan was to signify to the Jewish community that Jesus was and is the Son of God, therefore whatsoever Jesus asks the Father, He would do it. Jesus, aware of what is about to transpire, chooses to deny himself and follow the will of His Father knowing the end result will far exceed his physical death but will through agreement with the Father cause heaven and earth to accelerate God's plan to restore His righteous rule and save his people from their sins. Still Jesus chooses to agree with God. Let us begin with John 11:1-6:

Now a certain man was sick, named Lazarus, of Bethany, the town of Mary and her sister Martha. 2 (It was that Mary which anointed the Lord with ointment and wiped his feet with her hair whose brother Lazarus was sick.) 3 Therefore his sisters sent unto him, saying, Lord, behold he whom thou lovest is sick. 4 When Jesus heard that, he said, This sickness is not unto death but for the glory of God, that the Son of God might be glorified thereby. 5 Now Jesus loved Martha, and her sister, and Lazarus. 6 When he had heard therefore that he was sick, he abode two days still in the same place where he was (KJV).

Now if you read John Chapter 10 you will find it was only a short time before this, that Jesus miraculously escaped death by stoning while in Jerusalem. After that incident Jesus, moving by the authority of His Father, left that area only to be summoned back by Mary and Martha to help their brother Lazarus whom they stated was sick. The scripture specifically states, this was a family that Jesus loved. According to the way the world thinks, if you love someone you will rush to their rescue no matter what, simply because they are counting on you to save them. Jesus could not afford to think that way because He could not afford to be led by His emotions while He was striving to be in the perfect will of His Father. Yes, Jesus loved this family, but God so loved the world that He gave Jesus to die for the world to deliver us from sin. There is a lesson to be learned here, it is not about what we want Jesus to do for us, but it's about the will of God being done on the earth as it is in heaven. Father God cannot afford for our emotions to exceed His eternal purpose. This eternal purpose was established in the beginning. Psalms 100:3 says,

Know ye that the Lord he is God; it is he that hath made us, and not we ourselves; we are his people, and the sheep of his pasture (KJV).

We are God's idea, not the other way around. Keep in mind, we live in time and space; God does not. He created time and space, therefore, he can move in and out of it at His will. Father God sees our past, present and future all at the same time, He is omniscient. All we see is what we want, when we want it. Because of God's eternal purpose we must learn to trust and agree with Him no matter what. Let's continue with John 11:7-19.

7 Then after that saith he to his disciples, Let us go into Judea again. 8 His disciples say unto him, Master, the Jews of late sought to stone thee; and goest thou thither again. 9 Jesus answered, Are there not twelve hours in the day? If any man walk in the day, he stumbleth not, because he seeth the light of this world. 10 But if a man walk in the night, he stumbleth, because there is no light in him. 11 These things said he; and after that he saith unto them, Our friend Lazarus sleepeth; but I go that I may awake him out of sleep. 12 Then said his disciples, Lord, if he sleep, he shall do well. 13 Howbeit Jesus spake of his death; but they thought that he had spoken of taking of rest in sleep. 14 Then said Jesus unto them plainly, Lazarus is dead. 15 And I am glad for your sakes that I was not there, to the intent ye may be-lieve; nevertheless let us go unto him. 16 Then said Thomas, which is called Didymus, unto his fellow disciples, Let us also go that we may die with him. 17 Then when Jesus came, he found that he had lain in the grave four days already. 18 Now Bethany was nigh unto Jerusa-lem, about fifteen furlongs off: 19 And many of the Jews came to Mar-tha and Mary, to comfort them concerning their brother. (KJV)

It is important to consider who you surround yourself with during difficult times. The Bible does not say Mary and Martha sent for the Jews, it says the Jews came to them. As we continue to read we find Martha is still holding on to the fact when Jesus get here he can change things. But from the looks of the situation there is no one to agree with her. Remember many of the Jews did not believe on Jesus at this time. People of faith must surround themselves with people of like faith. We must be careful because if our faith is not anchored in Jesus, fear and doubt can shake it at its foundation. No matter what your situation may be, never allow negative talk, spirits of fear and disillusionment tear down what you know to be true and faithful about your Father God.

Continue reading John 11:

20 Then Martha, as soon as she heard that Jesus was coming went and met him; but Mary sat still in the house. Then said Martha unto Jesus, Lord, If thou hadst been here, my brother had not died. 22 **But I know,** *that even now, whatsoever thou wilt ask of God, God will give it thee. 23 Jesus saith unto her, Thy brother shall rise again. 24 Martha saith unto him, I know that he shall rise again in the resurrection at the last day. 25 Jesus said unto her, I am the resurrection, and the life: he that believeth in me, though he were dead, yet shall he live: 26 And whosoever liveth and believeth in me shall never die. Believest thou this?* (KJV)

Can you hear Jesus saying this to you right now? **"Can you believe I can still do this, if so, touch and agree with me?"** Don't spend precious time complaining about your situation or asking Jesus why he didn't do it your way, just touch and **agree with him now**. Matthew 18:20 says, *For where two or three are gathered together in my name, there am I in the midst of them* (KJV).

Let's continue with John 11:27,

27 She (Martha) saith unto him, Yea Lord: I believe that thou art the Christ, the Son of God, which should come into the world. 28 And when she had so said she went her way, and called Mary her sister secretly, saying, The Master is come, and calleth for thee (KJV).

Note: You can only call Him Master, when you agree with Him, no matter what!

29 As soon as she (Mary) heard that, she arose quickly and came unto him. 30 Now Jesus was not yet come into the town, but was in that place where Martha met him. 31 The Jews then which were with her in the house, and comforted her, when they saw Mary, that she rose up hastily and went out, followed her, saying, She goeth unto the grave to weep there. 32 Then when Mary was come where Jesus was, and saw him, she fell down at his feet, saying unto him, Lord, if thou hadst been here, my brother had not died. 33 When Jesus therefore saw her weeping, and the Jews also weeping which came with her, he groaned in the spirit, and was troubled (KJV).

I cannot tell you why Jesus groaned when he saw Mary. I can only speculate. The Bible tells us our thoughts and ways are as far from God's as the East is from the West, but when you have developed a personal relationship with God, you must learn to protect that union from fear, doubt and disbelief. You cannot allow yourself to be surrounded with fear and unbelievers and expect to step out on faith in God. God cannot agree with fear and doubt. Remember, without faith it is impossible to please God.

34 And (Jesus) said, Where have ye laid him? They said unto him, Lord, come and see. 35 Jesus wept. 36 Then said the Jews, Behold how he loved him! (KJV)

Did you notice here, when Jesus sees Mary, He does not take time to agree with her, but instead groans in the spirit when he sees her brokenness? He also can perceive the thoughts of those who have surrounded her. Look at verse 37,

37 And some of them said, Could not this man, which opened the eyes of the blind have caused that even this man should not have died? (KJV)

Is it possible they could have picked up on what Mary was thinking and openly rehearsed it before her? Remember faith cometh by hearing, but also fear, doubt and disbelief. But have no fear, for God knew this would happen from the very beginning. Let's look at **Luke 10: 38-42:**

Now it came to pass, as they went, that he (Jesus) entered into a certain village; and a certain woman named Martha received him into her house. **39 And she had a sister called Mary, which also sat at Jesus feet, and heard his word.** *40 But Martha was cumbered about much serving, and came to him and said Lord, dost thou not care that my sister hath left me to serve alone? Bid her therefore that she help me. 41 And Jesus answered and said unto her, Martha, Martha, thou art careful and troubled about many things; 42 But one thing is **needful**: and Mary hath chosen that good part, **which shall not be taken away from her** (KJV).*

Long before Lazarus became sick, the Father knew what would be needed to get this family through it. Remember, Jesus, the Father and the Holy Spirit are one. In the beginning, they knew what would happen to Lazarus and how Mary would become broken and disconnected because of it. Jesus knew Martha would be alright, but Mary would need to be reassured, therefore, **in the beginning,** faith and hope was set in motion in the form of a special visit to Martha and Mary's house long before Lazarus became sick. Jesus, during this visit, made provisions for Mary to sit at His feet and listen to His words. Because of Jesus's connection to God, He is already aware of Mary's state of mind during this upcoming crisis, therefore He allows for her to choose **that good part,** now, before the crisis takes place. This initial visit was not to come over their house for a home-cooked meal, but was an opportunity for Mary to sit in the presence of the Lord and receive healing for her soul. If you think about it, there has never been a time when the Holy Spirit did not try to call you aside to spend time with Him because God wanted to prepare you for your upcoming crisis. But God will not make us do anything, it is our choice to draw near or to walk away. If you are to make it through this next test you have got to make a conscious decision to spend time with Jesus. Only He knows where that weakened, empty, hurting place is within you and how to speak life, strength and determination into it. **Jesus said Mary had chosen** that good part (which was sitting in His presence), therefore he promised her, when the time comes and you need strength from me, "it would not be taken away from her."

Now back to John 11:38

38 Jesus therefore again groaning in himself cometh to the grave. It was a cave and a stone lay upon it, 39 Jesus said, Take ye away the stone. Martha, the sister of him that was dead, saith unto him, Lord, by this time he stinketh; for he hath been dead four days. 40 Jesus saith unto her, Said I not unto thee, that, if thou wouldest believe, thou shouldest see the glory of God? (KJV).

Note: Sometimes we have to be reminded of what we are agreeing with God about, especially, when faced with the realities of the situation. Just remember when these situation arise we must agree, quickly, before fear can get a foot hold.

41 Then they took away the stone from the place where the dead was laid. And Jesus lifted up his eyes, and said, Father, I thank thee that thou hast heard me. 42 And I knew that thou hearest me always; but because of the people which stand by I said it, that they may believe that thou hast sent me. 43 And when he thus had spoken, he cried with a loud voice, Lazarus, come forth. 44 And he that was dead came forth, bound hand and foot with grave clothes: and his face was bound about with a napkin. Jesus said unto them, Loose him and let him go (KJV).

Now let's pick up at John 12:1:

Then Jesus six days before the Passover came to Bethany, where Lazarus was which had been dead, whom he raised from the dead. 2 There they made him a supper; and Martha served: but Lazarus was one of them that sat at the table with him (KJV).

All right, get ready for this. We are back at Mary's side watching what she is about to do;

3 Then took Mary a pound of ointment of spikenard, very costly, and anointed the feet of Jesus and wiped his feet with her hair: and the house was filled with the odor of the ointment (KJV).

Wow, how beautiful this moment is when Mary pours her love for the Master from her box of alabaster. She did not stop to explain what she was doing or even why, but the one who needed to know, already knew. For it was Jesus who declared, "Mary has chosen that good part, and it shall not be taken away from her." Praise God forever!!! When did Jesus know this about Mary, Martha and Lazarus . . . "in the beginning."

HOW LONG ARE YOU WILLING TO SEARCH FOR GOD?

It is good for me that I have been afflicted; that I might learn thy stat-ue. Psalms 119:71 (KJV)

Searching the depths of God is rarely our idea. Usually, some-thing happens in our lives that causes us to cry out to God for help realizing we cannot make it on our own. But as we have already discussed, this search has already been ordained of God before the foundations of the earth and is needed for us to reach our full potential in Christ. I believe for everyone called and chosen of God there is a burning bush experience just waiting to be discovered. With this ex-perience comes a glimpse of His Majesty that stirs a desire within our very souls to run after the God who patiently waits for us. But what is He after?

When I first started teaching, I held conferences several times a year throughout the city. My messages were based on the God of the miraculous who would catch you before you could fall and heal you overnight. I was teaching my Jesus the way I had experienced Him up to that point in my life. He was the God of visions and supernatural encounters. During these conferences, I preached the God who had healed my acute back pain in just a matter of weeks contrary to the diagnoses stating the condition would be *crippling* and *debilitating*. I shared with people the God who had filled my savings account with more than enough and left my family wanting for nothing. I taught about the God who would never hide Himself from His people, but would come to their rescue with just the mention of the name of Jesus. I gave testimony how the Lord had me praying for my husband the night his 18 wheeler plunged into a ditch, long before I was notified of the situation by the company's dispatchers. I ministered to the people the God I knew who would deliver you before you could be thrown into the fiery furnace. Yes, I taught about the God of the suddenly and the instantaneous. Most of the people who would attend these conferences were young and spunky and would sit on the edge of their seats listening to the supernatural experiences the Lord had given me to share. I loved those conferences and thank Father God for affording me that opportunity to share my heart. I believe many were healed and blessed by the Power of God during those services. I was convinced I had found my purpose in life and that it was teaching the spontaneous "acts" of God. Wow, if I had only known where all of this was about to lead me.

After conducting these conferences for several years, I felt the leading of God to start spending more time at our home church helping build our ministry there. It felt good being back at our home base and the people seems to be prospering from the teaching and preaching of the Word of God. I thought God was allowing me an opportunity to get some rest from working so hard on the conferences, but the real reason for Him calling me home was to prepare me for some of the most difficult years of my life. Like a child sitting at the feet of the Father, my Jesus knew what I was about to step into and with my one dimensional experiences of Him, I would need to broaden my view of His capabilities in order to survive. He was calling me aside to pre-pare me for a deeper, more intimate walk with Him that would cause me to search for Him in a way I never thought possible. I would soon find out that as wonderful as the instantaneous works of God are, not everyone will receive what they are looking for that way. There was a deeper side of Him I needed to be able to relate to; a side that included healing as a process, one that required effectual and fervent prayer in order to receive a breakthrough. Yes, He is the God of the overnight spontaneous healings, but He is also the God who is well able to fashion each person's test and assignment to best fit and accomplish his overall will and plan for their lives. I had developed faith for the acute, instantaneous works of God, but now I would need to develop endurance for the chronic things that come to wear you down, drain your resources and cause you to lose hope and focus.

Take a moment to ponder the next three verses before proceeding.

Genesis 1:11 says,

*Then God said "let the earth bring forth grass, **the herb that yields** **seed**, and the fruit tree that yields fruit **according to its kind**, **whose** **seed is in itself**, on the earth"; and it was so* (NKJV).

Isaiah 53:10 says,

*Yet it pleased the Lord to bruise Him; He has put Him to grief. When You make His soul an offering for sin, **He shall see His seed, He shall** **prolong His days, And the pleasure of the Lord shall prosper in His** **hand*** (NKJV).

John 15: 1-2 says,

I AM the True Vine, and My Father is the Vinedresser.

*2 Any branch in Me that does not bear fruit [that stops bearing] He cuts away (trims off, takes away); and **He cleanses and repeatedly** **prunes every branch that continues to bear fruit to make it bear more** **and richer and more excellent fruit*** (AMP).

For over a year, I sensed the Lord calling me aside to pray more and spend time in His Presence. Oh how I wish I could have a "do over" regarding this opportunity of communion with the Father, because the situations I was about to be confronted with would require every ounce of grace, mercy and favor I could receive from Him. Within a year, I was diagnosed as an insulin dependent diabetic requiring me to take up to four injections a day. I was working as a registered nurse at the time and having to monitor my blood sugar levels and nutritional intake was a bit distracting. A week later while getting ready for work, I had a right-sided brain stroke. Now, instead of being the caregiver, I was receiving care from family and friends. Later that same year, I was in my office at work, when I collapse. One of my co-workers found me unconscious under my desk. After a hospitalization and many diagnostic test, I was diagnosed with a seizure disorder. Needless to say, that little incident cost me my job and freedom to drive. With all of this going on, I had no other choice but to ignore the skin lesions growing and covering my legs and feet. Through all of this, I rebuked the enemy and declared the power of God over my life. My constant prayer was, "Lord, please allow me to focus on you and your goodness and not be distracted by what is happening around me or to me." In a matter of months, I developed diabetic nerve pain along with sensory-motor polyneuropathy that required lots of bed-rest and pain medication. The pain was so intense it seemed to take on a personality of its own. At times I could visualize the pain as *a living, breathing thing* I had to burp and medicate on a regular basis. In the midst of all of this, I began to notice I was seeing everything in shadows. My vision was failing and everything I saw was cloaked in shades of gray. People and objects no longer had shape or depth. Although, I knew I needed to see someone regarding my deteriorating eyesight, the pain I was dealing with overruled any activity that called for me to move or change into clothing appropriate for such an occasion. The mere effort of getting up and going to the car for such an appointment was out of the question. Just when I thought things could not possible get any more intense, I had to be prepped for major corrective abdominal surgery. After the surgery, I discovered I had been under anesthesia so long, I was now being plagued with audible hallucinations. As the year progressed, I was able to add another major surgery, bilateral lenses replacements, multiple low back pain procedures, and a rotator cuff injury to the mix. Oh, and did I mention the two years of clinical depression that followed?

During this time I had so many people laying hands on me and praying for me, I felt like kneaded dough. Every time I picked up the Bible to read, I went straight to the Book of Job. (By the way, I have an entirely new respect for the Brother!) This may sound strange, but the longer I dealt with these afflictions the weaker my body appeared, but the stronger my faith and fight became. Every ailment that attacked my body, during those years, appeared as chronic and life-changing. My husband and I prayed constantly and sought God for total deliverance. The church started a prayer chain as well, but with all of this going on, I still had to wait for my change to come. I wish I could tell you I sang, danced and shouted my way through all of these afflictions, but it was not like that at all. I spent a lot of time crying, wallowing, vomiting, seizing, praying, and waiting for my breakthrough. It is one thing to go through such times behind closed doors, but because I was the one of the pastors of our church, my appointment called for me to have to sit on the stage, in front of the congregation, and continue to preach, teach, pray, prophesy, praise God and be an example of the believer I had been preaching about for years. Every Sunday I had to wait for my daughter to come to the house and help me get dressed while my husband waited on me and stayed by my side. When it was time for me to preach, I could hear the enemy telling me I was going to have a seizure or double over in pain, but without fail I could hear the Holy Spirit reminding me who I am in Christ and that I was never forgotten or alone. Although I hated every minute of this test I was in, I never felt alone or abandoned of God. I could always sense the presence of Jesus standing by me and whispering words of love and faith to me. With tears in my eyes, I found myself praying through-out the day, every day. At first my prayers were for me and my deliverance, then I noticed I began to pray for those who had been in pain, such as this, all of their lives with no relief in sight. I prayed for the lost, as well, as for the Body of Christ. I prayed until my focus was no longer on my pain and my needs, but the pain and needs of those who did not know God could heal them. I hate to admit it, but I had never prayed this long and diligently before for anyone or anything. In the midst of all this distress, Jesus was teaching me . . .

changing me . . . molding me into a new creature for His service.

As Isaiah 53:10 declares, there was a seed within me, placed there by God, and now He was after it.

Isaiah 53:10 says,

Yet it pleased the Lord to bruise Him; He has put Him to grief. When You make His soul an offering for sin, ***He shall see His seed, He shall prolong His days, And the pleasure of the Lord shall prosper in His hand*** (NKJV).

For years, my prayer had been to please the Lord. Not understanding what that really meant, I was expecting to sing and shout my way into His heart. I even preached how I would like to be like Enoch who pleased the Lord so much He was translated.

Hebrews 11:5,

Because of faith Enoch was caught up and transferred to heaven so that he did not have a glimpse of death; and he was not found, because God had translated him. For even before he was taken to heaven, he received testimony [still on record] that he had pleased and been satisfactory to God [Gen. 5:21-24](AMP).

For years I had assumed in order to please God all I had to do was go to church and live the best way I knew how. I had no idea God's good pleasure comes when He witnesses the maturation of the "seed" He has planted within us. The seed is that which produces after its own kind. Remember, God breathed into us His breath of life and man **became** a living soul. It is His seed that causes us to emulate His character and His ways and produces the fruit of the Spirit. I had been waiting for Him to heal my body, my outward man, my flesh. But God was after so much more. He was not just healing my body, but my soul and spirit. I did not realize I had a judgmental spirit until I felt the eyes of those watching me wondering why I had been plagued with such distress. Is that the same way I used to look at those whose plight I did not understand? The longer I was in this test, the more I learned to be silent and allow the Lord to show me myself. Even my prayers changed, instead of talking so much, I found myself sitting in His presence . . . waiting . . . listening. I was, finally, learning how to keep silent and allow God to minister His will into my life. Instead of Jesus having to wait for me to take time to come to Him, I found myself, chasing and searching after Him with all of my heart. I soon stopped searching for Him for my healing and I started running after Him just to hear Him speak my name, and I His. In my moments of weakness, I found His strength. When I wanted to give up and give in, I felt Him urging me to fight. As sick as I thought I was, I knew this thing had an ending to it, and that ending would include a closer walk and aware-ness of the Healer of my body and Savior of my soul.

You see, all of my life I had been asking God for a closer walk with Him. I had read about the things He had done in the lives of others, but I wanted my own love story with Him. I wanted my own experiences with Him. Knowing He is no respecter of persons, I wanted my time on the earth to please Him and show forth His glory to all who may not believe He is still Our Only Wise and True God. As a Bible teacher, I went about demonstrating the power of God by sharing His awesomeness and miracle working power through what I had perceived as His acts. But now I could sense through these trials, I was learning His ways. Although I had never admitted it, I could not understand why some people could not be healed as quickly as I had been in the past. Surely (I thought) they must not know the same God I know. Could it be they did not pray as long or worship Him with as much intimacy as I had? Maybe they had some sin or character issue that needed to be addressed. **How quickly we judge people and their circumstances, especially, when we have experienced only one**

side of God ourselves. I had no idea I had become so pious and religious. Because others were on a different path than my own, I considered they must not be living a righteous life. This kind of thinking can cause us to miss out on the fullness of what God desires to do within us. Sure you may be doing some wonderful things in the ministry in the eyes of man, but are you operating in the full potential of the anointing according to the expectations of the Holy Spirit of God. No matter how anointed you may feel, without the true character of the Father and evidence of the Fruit of the Spirit you will not please God. (Thank God for His patience with us while we are on the potter's wheel. I had so much to learn about God and His actions and ways.) Who knew within a matter of years, I would be one of the ones who had to wait and endure suffering as a good soldier while, all the time, refusing to give up and die?

Anyone can serve, preach, teach and testify about Him when it's just a pop quiz, but when it's time for the real exam, we must be able, to not only walk through the fire; but battle the flames. He is training us to swim through the flood; while battling the sharks that come to devour. He wants us to know that no matter how things may appear, Our Father is well able to deliver and make us overcomers through it all. How can I tell others He is a deliverer when I have not experienced Him at my side while I am being delivered? Yes, He is the Healer of the acute illnesses and injuries, but, also, of the chronic, debilitating afflictions.

I can still remember when my healing started to manifest. I was getting ready for a doctor's appointment when I began to sense a change in the atmosphere. I turned around and looked at my bed and noticed there was someone lying there. As I stared at the figure, I noticed it was an elderly woman lying on her right side in a fetal position. I stood watching her as she slowly moved her fingers, but it was obvious she could not move any other parts of her body. Who was this woman and how did she get in our house . . . in our bed? I remember taking a step towards the bed to see if I recognized her, and to my surprise it was an older, debilitated version of myself. Can you believe that? In the midst of everything I was already dealing with, demonic forces had set up this vision for me to accept as my expected end. Although I was getting dressed to go to the doctor's office, when I saw this vision, I straightened my back and went to war. I declared who I am in the Lord and spoke His words over my life. I spoke in my heavenly language and worshiped and praised my God until the vision was no longer visible. By the time the Holy Spirit was through with me, I felt like running a marathon. What the enemy meant for bad, God had allowed me the strength to turn it around. Thank you Jesus! From that moment on, I began to sense my deliverance coming into view. Praise God Forever!

Today I am a new creature inside and out. I never would have chosen this route to a closer walk with God, but now that I have survived it, I would not exchange the experience for anything in the world. I have come out of this situation healed and completely whole. Many have ask me what lesson I have learned through all of this. I would say, I am no longer afraid of the hard things in life, I am no longer afraid to open the door to the unexpected and most of all, I no longer tell God what I can't do or what I can't take, because with Him I can do it all.

Please understand, I am not saying God placed these things on me, but I believe He allowed me to go this route to strengthen me and intensify my relationship with Him. There were things I needed to know about Him I could not read in a book. Things that only could be obtained through daily communion, fasting and prayer with the Lover of our souls. Only Father God knows what He is after in us, therefore we must be willing to sign up for the class, trust the Instructor and pass the test.

What seed is He after in you?

DEEP CALLS UNTO DEEP

Yet it pleased the Lord to bruise Him; He has put Him to grief. When You make His soul an offering for sin, He shall see His seed, He shall prolong His days, And the pleasure of the Lord shall prosper in His hand (NKJV).

Isaiah 53:10

In this passage, the prophet Isaiah talks about how Jesus would be perceived by others as He walked upon the earth. Jesus, in His divinity, made a conscious decision to humble Himself and dwell among His creations. Because He was given as a gift unto men, by the Father, Jesus chose to become obedient to His enemy (death) in order to save us. Jesus, in all of His glory, chose to please the Father and submit Himself to the death of the cross.

Philippians 2:5-8

Let this mind be in you, which was also in Christ Jesus: 6 Who, being in the form of God, thought it not robbery to be equal with God: 7 But made himself of no reputation and took upon him the form of a servant, and was made in the likeness of men: 8 And being found in fashion as a man, he humbled himself and became obedient unto death, even the death of the cross (KJV).

Jesus, who is already Righteous and who is already loved of the Father, chose to take on the sins of man that we might be made the Righteousness of God.

2 Corinthians 5:21,

For he hath made him to be sin for us, who knew no sin; that we might be made the righteousness of God in him (KJV).

Jesus knew who He was, but the assignment called for Him to submit Himself to the will of the Father. Can you imagine having created the universe and all therein, then purposefully yielding to the death of the cross by the hands of those you had created? To walk among the creatures (mankind) and they not recognize you; to sit among men who wanted you to prove to them you are who you say you are, only to mock and spit in your face as they deliberately caused you bodily harm and disgrace. Jesus was willing to do all of this, not only for us, but for His Father's pleasure. Ironically, although the creature (mankind) did not recognize who Jesus was, all of creation was well aware of His presence on the earth. Let's examine the following scriptures:

Mark 4:36-41 is a perfect example of this,

And when they had sent away the multitude, they took him even as he was in the ship. And there were also with him other little ships.

37 And there arose a great storm of wind, and the waves beat into the ship, so that it was now full.

38 And he was in the hinder part of the ship, asleep on a pillow: and they awake him, and say unto him, Master, carest thou not that we perish?

39 And he arose, and rebuked the wind, and said unto the sea, Peace, be still. And the wind ceased, and there was a great calm.

40 And he said unto them, Why are ye so fearful? How is it that ye have no faith?

41 And they feared exceedingly, and said one to another, What manner of man is this that even the wind and the sea obey him?(KJV).

How quickly the winds and waves obeyed their Master's voice. Although mankind may say, "there is no God," all of creation continues to declare His glory and Righteous Rule as they continue to be fruitful and multiply. Look at the story of the fig tree:

Matthew 21:18-20,

18 Now in the morning as he returned into the city, he hungered.

19 And when he saw a fig tree in the way he came to it, and found nothing thereon, but leaves only, and said unto it, Let no fruit grow on thee henceforth forever. And presently the fig tree withered away.

20 And when the disciples saw it, they marveled, saying, How soon is the fig tree withered away! (KJV)

All it took for the fig tree, winds and waves to respond to the commands of Jesus, was to hear His voice. Yet the religious sect of that day and the unbelievers chose to watch Him die rather than admit who He really was. We must remember, although Jesus was wrapped in flesh, He was still the Son of God. He was in constant contact with the Father and not only knew the scriptures, but was the Living Word all by Himself. He knew in His divinity (as the Son of God) He had declared,

Psalms 91:10-12,

There shall no evil befall thee, neither shall any plague come nigh thy dwelling. 11 For he shall give his angels charge over thee to keep thee in all thy ways. 12 They shall bear thee up in their hands, lest thou dash thy foot against a stone (KJV).

But in His humanity He knew and perceived the thoughts of others saying,

Matthew 27:42-43

42 He saved others; himself he cannot save. If he be the King of Israel, let him now come down from the cross, and we will believe him.

43 He trusted in God; let him deliver him now, if he will have him: for he said, I am the Son of God (KJV).

Here the scriptures states the angels are at his beck and call to keep him from harm, but Jesus shows us in order to please the Father we must be willing to be ridiculed and taunted by the enemy, yet stay focused on the Will of the Father. Throughout your trials and tribulations, you may hear many whispers and taunts from the enemy saying, "If you were living right you wouldn't be going through all of this." Others may slide up beside you and prophesy saying, "The Lord says you must repent for your wrong doings." All of these are distractions of the enemy to make you doubt God and lose focus. The enemy is after your hope. Your hope is the bases of your faith. You must not give in to these lies and strategies of the evil one. Remember, Jesus is our perfect example. **We must know beyond a shadow of a doubt, there is a seed of God within us that has been fashion to help us reach our expected end in God.**

Genesis 1:11 says,

*Then God said "let the earth bring forth grass, **the herb that yields seed**, and the fruit tree that yields fruit **according to its kind, whose seed is in itself**, on the earth"; and it was so* (NKJV).

This seed starts out as a small grain-like thought, but as it is revealed and grows within you, it allows you to become recognizable as a son of God.

1 John 3:2,

Beloved now we are the sons of God, and it doth not yet appear what we shall be: but we know that, when he shall appear, we shall be like him; for we shall see him as he is (KJV).

Mark 4: 28-29,

For the earth yields crops by itself: first the blade, then the head, after that the full grain in the head. 29 But when the grain ripens, immediately he puts in the sickle, because the harvest has come" (NKJV).

Let us examine

Isaiah 53:10 (KJV)

*Yet it pleased the Lord to bruise Him; He has put Him to grief. When You make His soul an offering for sin, **He shall see His seed**, He shall prolong His days, And the pleasure of the Lord shall prosper in His hand* (NKJV).

This scripture is not saying the Father is some cruel puppet master looking to make an example of those who will not yield to what He says. No, just the opposite. From the beginning the Father saw our end and has declared victory for all through the assignments He has fashioned for each of us to complete. The Father knows which of us are unstable and which are double-minded in our thinking. He is aware of those willing to walk out on Him and His salvation just because they did not get some monetary enticement for which they thought they were entitled. He, also, knows which ones are steadfast, unmovable and willing to go through the death of an entire family, the raping of a child, the agony of abandonment, and the cruelty of separation; and, not once, charge Him foolishly. The Father is well aware of it all, and is there to walk each of us through whatever obstacles that may arise.

There is nothing that surprises God. He is able to discern our thought and the intents of our hearts. He knows what you are capable of handling and what you believe will tear you apart. Therefore, the Father gives grace and mercy to those who cry out for Him. Remember, Father God sees everything about us, our past, present and future all at the same time. We live in time and space, He does not.

God is Omniscient (all knowing). He knew Aaron's character flaws from the beginning and that Moses did not need him for the task of delivering the children of Israel from Egypt. But because of Moses' insistence, God allowed Aaron to accompany Moses. God knew there was so much more to the assignment that He had given Moses

115

and that, eventually, Aaron would become more of a hinder than of an asset. We must remember, God will not go against our will or choices but patiently wait on us to come to know and trust Him. Although God knew Aaron would cause conflict along the way He, also, knew Moses needed a tangible person to lean on. Therefore God allowed Aaron to remain at Moses side until Moses learned to trust the voice of the God who called and chose him over any other influence sent to distract him.

God knows everything about us and the capabilities of the seed He has placed within us. He already has seen our end from the beginning and provisions have been made for every obstacle that may come our way. God made provisions for those who would live before the Cross and for us on this side of the Cross. All of this is visible on that screen I keep talking about from which Our Father sees our past, present and future in a glance. Father God already knew what Adam, Noah, Abraham, Daniel, David and Samuel would do long before they were born. He also knew of the ones who would make sacrifices for Him before receiving the promise, but were willing to endure trials and tribulations to show forth their faith in God. Those who according to Hebrews 11:33-40,

. . . through faith subdued kingdoms, worked righteousness, obtained promises, stopped the mouths of lions,

34 quenched the violence of fire, escaped the edge of the sword, out of weakness were made strong, became valiant in battle turned to flight the armies of the aliens.

These mighty saints of God must have known of the seed planted within them by the Father and longed to bring it forth for the Glory of God. How about verses 35-39,

35 Women received their dead raised to life again. Others were tortured, not accepting deliverance, that they might obtain a better resurrection.

36 *Still others had trial of mockings and scourgings, yes, and of chains and imprisonment.*

37 *They were stoned, they were sawn in two, were tempted, were slain with the sword. They wandered about in sheepskins and goatskins, being destitute, afflicted, tormented—*

38 *Of whom the world was not worthy. They wandered in deserts and mountains, in dens and caves of the earth.*

39 *And all these, having obtained a good testimony through faith, did not receive the promise,*

40 *God having provided something better for us that they should not be made perfect apart from us* (NKJV).

Jesus also knew of the covenant he had made with the Father regarding the salvation of all those who believed on Him.

John 3:16,

For God so loved the world, that he gave his only begotten Son, that whosoever believeth in him should not perish, but have everlasting life (KJV).

Some may think it was a dilemma for Jesus, knowing he had options, but no, He already had made up His mind what He would do. He would please the Father.

John 18:4-5,

*Jesus therefore, knowing all things that should come upon him, went forth, and said unto them, Whom seek ye? 5 They answered him, Jesus of Nazareth. Jesus saith unto them, **I am he**. And Judas also, which betrayed him, stood with them* (KJV).

When Jesus knew His hour had come, He was not about to deny who He was. It was not the Son of Man who was ready to please the

Father that night, for the flesh struggles to submit to the will of God; but it was the Son of God who submitted Himself to the will of the Father so that we would know how to respond **now that our hour is upon us**. Thank God for Jesus who allowed us to see his humanity in the midst of His divinity.

Luke 22:42,

Father, if thou be willing, remove this cup from me: **nevertheless not my will, but thine, be done** (KJV).

So often we say, "It's not about us", but do we really mean it? Some-time along this journey of life, difficult times will come and your faith will be tested. Everything we are asked to believe on this Christian journey has to do with the unseen. It is only when the unseen things of this life become more real than the tangible that we know our faith has matured. For without faith it is impossible to please God. Your actions speak so much louder than your words. Jesus through His sufferings taught us how to trust in the Lord, no matter what. Jesus yielded to the cross knowing He would rise again, not by His own might, but that of the Father. He already knew what the Father was capable of, but because He wanted us to know, he endured the cross . . . all for the joy of pleasing the Father. What is God asking you to endure and believe Him for?

Hebrews 12:2,

. . . (Jesus) *who for the joy that was set before Him endured the cross, despising the shame, and has sat down at the right hand of the throne of God* (NKJV).

THE SEARCH FOR THE HIDDEN THINGS OF GOD

Once I received the revelation of what God said "in the beginning", the Holy Spirit began to bring to my remembrance things spoken to me years ago. A few weeks after my husband and I were called to pastor I was taking an afternoon nap in our den. I was home alone but was awaken by these words,

"If you abide in me, and my words abide in you, you can ask what you will and it will be done unto you."

Now remember I was in nursing school at the time and had a lot on my mind, but when I heard these words and that voice, I knew it was the Lord. I am embarrassed now to admit this, but as I sat up on the couch I said, "I know that scripture. Those words are in the bible . . . but where?" I immediately got up and ran to my bedroom to get my bible and as soon as I opened it, it opened to John 15:7 which says,

"If ye abide in me, and my words abide in you, ye shall ask what ye will, and it shall be done unto you." (KJV)

I wanted to pinch myself to make sure I was awake. The Holy Spirit had spoken these words to me. Why me? I sat and pondered the message for a while before I told my husband later that day. Just like most of us, I disregarded the first portion of the verse and concentrated on the part stating "you shall ask what you will and it shall be done unto you." Thinking I had been given a license to shop and wish for whatever I fancied, I remember spending months naming and claiming, hoping and wishing; all to no avail. Before long I gave up on the thought of receiving such an amazing declaration from God and resumed my normal activities.

I soon realized if I did not seek the Lord regarding what He had spoken to me, I would miss one of the most important lessons I could ever know. I soon received this revelation of what He was showing me. If I would choose to become "One" with Him and His will, I could ask what I "will" and it would be done unto me. Once I became One with Him, in other words agreed with Him, there would be only One Will . . . the Will of the Father. Now the Holy Spirit was bringing this revelation back to me for a reason.

I had just received word a friend of mine had been diagnose with a life-threatening illness. Just as I was about to pray, I heard the same words as before. Ask what you will . . . and it shall be done unto you. I felt as though I had been reenergized with the Power of the Holy Spirit. I asked the Lord to heal my friend and just like He said, it was done. Could it be that easy, I thought? Then I remembered the revelation about "In the beginning . . ." and it all made sense. All I was doing was agreeing with what God had already said about this time in that person's life. My job was to agree with what God had already said and done in the beginning.

Genesis chapter one says God created man in His image and likeness. We are in the image and likeness of our Father who spoke everything into existence. Being created in His image and likeness and given the authority to take dominion over the earth gives us the license to act like Our Father. In order to restore the righteous rule back to God we must step into the role Our Father has set before us. The Kingdom of God is the logic of God. It is God's understanding of how He designed things to be. It is His way of utilizing what He has created, in other words, it is His purpose in practice. According to Daniel C. Rhodes author of *The Logos of the Kingdom (2014),*

"Spiritual Authority is the Power of Righteous Rule that emanates from God Himself. God alone possesses ultimate authority in both heaven and on earth. He rules with righteousness and justice and there is no darkness in Him. Yet, in God's unimaginable grace, He has cho-sen to share His authority with His redeemed community (His Church) and trust us to accomplish His work on earth. From a human perspec-

tive, the Spiritual Authority we have is a delegated assignment from God to represent the righteous cause of His Kingdom and to influence people for Christ in the earth! Those in whom the Lord has deposited His authority are accountable to Him to exercise that authority according to His character and purposes." (Rhodes, 2014, p 24.)

In Mark chapter 11, Jesus teaches us the importance of having God-like faith.

23 For verily I say unto you, that whosoever shall say unto this mountain, Be thou removed and be thou cast into the sea; and shall believe that those things which he saith shall come to pass; Therefore I say unto you, What things soever ye desire, when ye pray, believe that you receive them, and ye shall have them (KJV).

I am not saying that everything we pray for will come to pass, what I am saying is when we pray in agreement with the Word (Jesus) has already performed from what the Father has spoken in the beginning, God's Higher Purpose will prevail. Since we do not know what that Higher Purpose is, our job is to agree with what God has already spoken. When we know we belong to God and are the called according to His purpose, we can rest in Job 23:14 which says,

He (God) performeth the thing that is appointed unto me and many such things are with Him (KJV).

Mark chapter 11 verse 23 mentions how we can speak to the mountain and tell it to be removed and cast it into the sea and if we believe it shall be so. You may ask, "How can this be?" Let's look at Genesis 1:26-28

*26 And God said, Let us make man in our image, after our likeness; **and let them have dominion over the fish of the sea,** and **over the fowl of the air,** and over the cattle, and **over all the earth,** and over every creeping thing that creepeth upon the earth. 27 So God created*

man in his own image, in the image of God created he him; male and
female created he them. 28 And God blessed them and God said unto
them, Be fruitful, and multiply, and **replenish the earth, and subdue it;**
and have dominion over the fish of the sea, and over the fowl of the air
and **over every living thing that moveth upon the earth** (KJV).

Did you get that? God said if it is living and moves on upon the earth
we have dominion over it if we agree with what Our Father said in the
beginning.

According to **Isaiah 46:9-11** what God said in the beginning is still
reverberating now,

9 Remember the former things of old; for I am God and there is
none else; I am God and there is none like me, 10 Declaring the end
from the beginning, and from ancient times the things that are not
yet done saying, My counsel shall stand, and I will do all my plea-
sure: 11 Calling a ravenous bird from the east, the man that execu-
teth my counsel from a far country; yea, I have spoken it, I will also
bring it to pass; I have purposed it, I will also do it. (KJV).

Verse 10 does not say God declared it as in past tense, but it says
declaring the end from the beginning from ancient times the things
that are not yet done. God's Word is so potent that when He speaks
it, it has no end. The Word is Jesus who declares He is the Alpha and
Omega. The end the Father is declaring is out of time and space while
we live in time and space. What we consider the end is different from
His end because He is Eternal!

Verse 11 says He is able to call a ravenous bird from the east (to do His
bidding). Is that what happened to Elijah at the brook Cherith during
the famine? (1 Kings 173-6). This same verse states God can call a
man that executeth my counsel from a far country. Could that include
the vision Paul receives in Acts 16:9 when *"There stood a man of*
Macedonia, and prayed him, saying, Come over into Macedonia and

help us? God knows what is needed in the earth and who He can trust to execute these things. God is not holding His breath waiting to see what happens, He already has the plan in place. Our job as the Church of God is to develop an ear to hear what the Spirit is saying to us. Remember to everything there is a time and a season to every purpose under the heavens. You won't be able to agree with God if you can't hear what He is saying.

Let's look at Mark 4:37-40

And there arose a great storm of wind, and the waves beat into the ship, so that it was now full. 38 And he (Jesus) was in the hinder part of the ship, asleep on a pillow; and they awake him, and say unto him Master, carest thou not that we perish? 39 And he arose, and rebuke the wind, and said unto the sea, Peace, be still. And the wind ceased, and there was a great calm. 40 And he said unto them, Why are ye so fearful? How is it that ye have no faith? 41 And they feared exceedingly, and said one to another, What manner of man is this, that even the wind and the sea obey him? (KJV)

In case you missed that, remember Genesis 1:28b declares,

*And have dominion over the fish of the sea, and over the fowl of the air and **over every living thing that moveth upon the earth** (KJV).*

. . . the wind and the waves **were moving on the earth**. In other words, this principle of God works with all of creation. Jesus is the Son of God but when He was on the earth He referred to Himself as the Son of man, as well. This lets us know as long as we are on the earth and belong to God we, too, can walk in this agreement of authority. This principle is seen throughout the bible in the Old and New Testaments.

I have often wondered why God's encounter with Moses during the burning bush experience seemed to take so long. Exodus chapter 3 shows how God introduces Himself to Moses and discusses the assignment set before him. During this conversation we hear Moses continually telling God how he cannot do this because of his flaws and inadequacies, but God allows Him to stay close to Him and continues the conversation no matter how long it takes. What I could not understand then, I can see clearly now. The more time Moses spends with God the easier it is for Him to know His voice and His heart and to agree with Him in faith. The success of Moses's mission has its bases in Moses being able to hear the voice of God and act upon it correctly no matter what distractions may come his way. God already knows when Moses leads the people out of Egypt there will be a mixed multitude of people; many voices speaking contrary to what God has willed. This would not be the time for Moses to be guessing or supposing the will of God. Moses has to be on point without hesitation when God speaks to him the instructions for the people.

Read Exodus 14: 10-18 with me:

10 And when Pharaoh drew nigh, the children of Israel lifted up their eyes, and behold, the Egyptians marched after them; and they were sore afraid; and the children of Israel cried out unto the Lord. 11 And they said unto Moses, Because there were no graves in Egypt, hast thou taken us away to die in the wilderness? Wherefore hast thou dealt thus with us, to carry us forth out of Egypt? 12 Is not this the word that we did tell thee in Egypt, saying, Let us alone, that we may serve the Egyptians? For it had been better for us to serve the Egyptians than that we should die in the wilderness (KJV).

Can you imagine the sound of the voices of doubt surrounding Moses during this time? God knew what Moses would have to deal with therefore He allowed Moses to spend as much time as necessary in His presence. There are situation we will be sent

into where confusion and turmoil fill the atmosphere. This is why it is important to spend time with God so He can strengthen the weak places within us and give us peace. In times such as this you cannot enter the situation asking a lot of questions because God is sending you as the Answer. Let us continue:

13 And Moses said unto the people, Fear ye not, stand still, and see the salvation of the Lord, which he will shew to you today: for the Egyptians whom ye see today, ye shall see them again no more forever. 14 The Lord shall fight for you, and ye shall hold your peace. 15 And the Lord said unto Moses, Wherefore criest thou unto me? Speak unto the children of Israel that they go forward: 16 But lift thou up thy rod, and stretch out thine hand over the sea, and divide it: and the children of Israel shall go on dry ground through the midst of the sea. 17 And I, behold, I will harden the hearts of the Egyptians, and they shall follow them: and I will get me honor upon Pharaoh, and upon all his host, upon his chariots, and upon his horsemen. 18 And the Egyptians shall know that I am the Lord, when I have gotten me honor upon Pharaoh, upon his chariots and upon his horsemen (KJV).

Now, as Moses hears the instructions from God it is important for Him to stay focused because there are several things about to happen that Moses has never seen or experienced before. Moses cannot afford to appear confused or weak before the people or the enemy coming after them. It is not difficult to be confident when you know beyond a shadow of a doubt you are hearing from God and that it is not up to you to make this happen but up to the God who has called and chosen you for such a time as this. Let us continue:

19 And the angel of God, which went before the camp of Israel, removed and went behind them; and the pillar of the cloud went from before their face, and stood behind them: 20 And it came between the camp of the Egyptians and the camp of Israel; and it was a cloud of darkness to them, but it gave light by night to these: so that the one came not near the other all the night. 21 And Moses stretched out his hand over the sea; and the Lord caused the sea to go back by a strong east wind all that night, and made the sea dry land and the waters were divided. 22 And the children of Israel went into the midst of the sea upon the dry ground; and the waters were a wall unto them on their right hand, and on their left. 23 And the Egyptians pursued, and went in after them to the midst of the sea, even all Pharaoh's horses, his chariots and his horsemen. 24 And it came to pass, that in the morning watch the Lord looked unto the host of the Egyptians through the pillar of fire and of the cloud, and troubled the host of the Egyptians, 25 And took off their chariot wheels, that they drave them heavily: so that the Egyptians said, Let us flee from the face of Israel; for the Lord fighteth for them against the Egyptians (KJV).

Can you see how smoothly everything can go when you know you are in the perfect will of God? Now Moses can see why it took 80 years of heart break, frustration and isolation before he could know the answers to the questions in his heart. For every great move of God, there is a chosen vessel who must yield to the preparation needed to fulfill that assignment. Remember, many are called, but few are chosen.

This is a word for us right now. Many of you are wondering why you haven't been able to do the things for God you feel in your spirit you have been ordained to do. You are frustrated because of the isolation and many of you are determined to break out and make things happen on your own. But the bible tells us many times "He who has an ear to hear, let him hear what the Spirit says to the churches." Only God knows what surrounds your assignment. Remember we often see only one side of the situation while our multi-dimensional God sees and know everything that awaits us. More happens to us than we know when we are in the presence of God. Many think because they are not feeling goose bumps up and down their spine that God is not doing anything. You are so wrong. We must stop and recognize more happens in the spirit realm than in the natural realm. Once I asked the Holy Spirit about the feast and famine experiences when I go into my prayer closet to pray. I asked why sometimes I would feel the anointing all over me just by whispering the name of Jesus, while other times it seemed as though no one was listening at all. This is what I heard Him say,

"There is never a time you draw near to Me when I am not already there to meet you. Always remember, so much more happens than you can sense or imagine. That is why you must walk by faith, not by sight. Without faith, it is impossible to please Me. Even when you think I am not listening, I am there filling you with wisdom, while fortifying your weakened places and preparing you for the times ahead. There is never wasted time in the presence of the Lord."

SEARCHING BEYOND YOUR POINT OF REFERENCE

In this section we want to discuss the importance of prayer and intercession. In previous chapters we have discussed importance of agreeing with the Father regarding what we should say and believe. Jesus prayed in John Chapter 17 that we be one with the Father as He (Jesus) is one. It is in that oneness that we develop the mind of Christ and walk in the perfect will of God.

Webster's New World College Dictionary defines the word intercede as:

- To plead or make a request in behalf of another or others

- To intervene for the purpose of producing agreement; meditate

Using the same source, prayer is defined as:

- An earnest request; entreaty

- A humble and sincere request as unto God

- An utterance as unto God, in praise, thanksgiving confession, etc

It is a privilege and honor to be able to approach the throne of God and pray to our Father. Because of the redemptive work of Our Lord Jesus, we are at liberty to approach the throne of God anytime and He is there to hear, love, and minister into us in ways we may never understand. But how many of us take full advantage of this blessed gift from God? Just to know the God of all creation has provided an intimate, unlimited access for His children to approach Him is one of the mysteries of the ages we may never fully comprehend. To add to this wonder, we are told to boldly approach Him knowing no matter how many other people are calling on Him, He is still able to recognize each of us as individuals. As we grow in the knowledge of God, we must always remember the price that has been paid for the privilege of coming before the Father in prayer. As we pray to Our Father, Jesus our High Priest makes intercessions for us helping us to obtain mercy and find grace to help in the time of need.

Hebrews 4: 14-16,

Seeing then that we have a great High Priest who has passed through the heavens, Jesus the Son of God, let us hold fast our confession. 15 For we do not have a High Priest who cannot sympathize with our weaknesses, but was in all points tempted as we are, yet without sin. 16 Let us therefore come boldly to the throne of grace that we may obtain mercy and find grace to help in time of need (NKJV).

We are the Body of Christ and have been given the assignment to take back dominion from the evil one and restore the Righteous Rule of the Father on earth as it is in heaven. Therefore, when we pray we must pray with this mandate in mind. Understandably, when we first receive salvation, we are uncertain about what Our Father requires of us. We go to church and read the Bible, but we are not sure how to pray as we ought. This is why it is imperative we seek the guidance of the Holy Spirit of God. Without the guidance of the Holy Spirit, we may have the tendency to pray out of our weaknesses, therefore praying for the add-on instead of the things pertaining to the Kingdom of God. What are "add-on"? Look at Luke 12:29-31,

*"And do not seek what you should eat or what you should drink, nor have an anxious mind. 30 For all these things the nations of the world seek after, and your Father knows that you need these things. 31 But seek the kingdom of God, and **all these things shall be added to you*** (NKJV)".

How often do we bombard heaven praying for the necessities of this life? The scriptures tell us Our Father is well aware that we have need of these things. But is this the reason Jesus gave His life, so we could pray for enough money to pay our light bills?

Matthew 5:7-9,

When you pray, don't babble on and on as people of other religions do. They think their prayers are answered merely by repeating their words again and again. 8 Don't be like them, for your Father knows exactly what you need even before you ask him! (NIV).

We cannot continue to come into His presence with a laundry list of 'wants' and 'gotta haves', but recognize who we are in the Body of Christ and pray with the Will of God in mind. When we pray using carnal knowledge and not from our spirit, we are praying out of our weaknesses. But remember the Father has given us all the help we need to overcome those weaknesses and to pray the will of the Father.

Romans 8:26

Likewise the Spirit also helps in our weaknesses. *For we do not know what we should pray for as we ought, but the Spirit Himself makes intercession for us with groanings which cannot be uttered* (NKJV).

Hebrews 4:15,

15 For we do not have a High Priest who cannot sympathize with our weaknesses, *but was in all points tempted as we are, yet without sin* (NKJV).

Jesus says in John 14:13,

And whatever you ask in My name, that I will do, that the Father may be glorified in the Son. 14 If you ask anything in My name, I will do it (NKJV).

When we enter into prayer, we must learn to listen as well as speak to

God. Allow the Holy Spirit to direct your words and actions when you are in the presence of the Lords.

Ecclesiastes 5:1-2 says,

Walk prudently when you go to the house of God; and draw near to hear rather than to give the sacrifice of fools, for they do not know that they do evil. 2 Do not be rash with your mouth And let not your heart utter anything hastily before God. For God is in heaven, and you on earth; Therefore let your words be few (NIV).

As we search for the depths of God, we soon realize we are unable to continue to pray the prayers of babes in Christ. In other words, we must evolve in our thinking and mature in our spirits to allow the Holy Spirit to instruct us what the Father is in need of. The Bible teaches us how, as children of God, we do not know how to pray as we should, therefore we must follow the unction of the Holy Spirit for guidance to the will of the Father.

PRACTICAL APPLICATIONS OF SPIRIT LED PRAYERS

So he commanded the chariot to stand still. And both Philip and the eunuch went down into the water, and he baptized him. 39 **Now when they came up out of the water, the Spirit of the Lord caught Philip away,** *so that the eunuch saw him no more; and he went on his way rejoicing. 40 But Philip was found at Azotus. And passing through, he preached in all the cities till he came to Caesarea* (NKJV).

Acts 8:38-40

We must remember, when we are involved in Spirit led prayers, many times we may not understand the situation and all of the details are rarely given to us. This is why we are called to walk by faith and not by sight. Our job is to follow the leading of the Spirit of God and lean not to our own understanding. I will not reveal names of the people involved in these situations, but I want to give you examples of what the Holy Spirit may expect of us as the Body of Christ when we become one with the Father.

IN NEED OF A BREAKTHROUGH

While washing dishes one evening, I felt the leading of the Holy Spirit to pray. I stopped what I was doing and went to my prayer closet. While on my knees, I saw a woman mopping a floor in a large hallway off from a larger room with rectangular tables and folding chairs. The woman was medium complexion, with shoulder length dark wavy hair pulled back in a ponytail. She wore a light blue shirt tucked into dark blue pants. As she continued to mop the floor a guard came to her and told her she had to go to her cell. Without much dis-cussion, she went to the cell and as soon as the doors shut, she walked over to a bottom bunk, fell on her knees and began to pray. It was then I felt her burden. While watching her, I noticed tears streaming down her face as she began a whispered prayer to God. Without understand-ing what was going on, I found myself praying with her. I felt the Holy

Spirit leading me to agree with her in prayer, so I did. She spoke in a language foreign to my natural mind, but familiar in the spirit realm. After praying for about 20 minutes, she wiped her tears, and stood up. The guard came to the cell and told her she could resume her duties. With a slight smile on her face she went back to mopping the floor and I felt the burden leave me. I began to rejoice in the Spirit knowing what she had asked of the Lord was now done.

PRAY FOR PEACE

While in prayer one evening, I noticed I was speaking in a language I had never experienced before. The next thing I knew, I found myself walking in the midst of a group of about 30 to 40 men, women and children. Many were carrying bundles on their backs and atop their heads and the children were in their bare feet. The women wore head coverings and the men were in frayed trousers and few had on shirts. They were not speaking to each other but chanting as a group as they walked down this narrow dirt road. It was in the evening and the weather was hot and the insects torturous. As before, I could see and hear them, but they were not aware I was there. After speaking the words with them, I heard the Holy Spirit say, "Pray for Peace for them and this country." As they continued on their journey I began to speak peace over the land. I prayed for the families and relatives as led by the Holy Spirit and afterwards I found myself back on my face in my prayer closet.

THE SEARCH PARTY

A few weeks ago, I was putting the grocery up in the pantry when I received an unction from the Holy Spirit to go into my prayer closet. Once there, I received a vision of men and women, some in of-

ficial uniforms, others in plain clothes, walking in a straight line over rough terrain. In the background I heard dogs barking and people calling out a name. I recognized the scene as that of a search party and I found myself yielding to the Holy Spirit as to how to pray. As they were walking, I found myself praying because the people were calling out a specific name of a lost child, but could not hear a response. Not understanding what had just happened, I stayed on my knees until I received a release from the Holy Spirit of God.

LEAN NOT TO YOUR OWN UNDERSTANDING

Romans 11:33

Oh, the depth of the riches both of the wisdom and knowledge of God! How unsearchable are His judgements and His ways past finding out!

Our God is an Awesome God! He is full of wisdom and knowledge. He knows where we are at all times and watches over His word to perform it. There may be times you are ask to pray for people or situations and find yourself hesitant because of the way the Holy Spirit presents it to you. The following is a perfect example of the importance of speaking and praying the way you are instructed by the Spirit of God, leaning not to your own understanding. Remember, we are His people and the sheep of His pastures. Be quick to obey His word just as He speaks it into your spirit.

Several years ago, my husband and I were packing our suitcases for the drive to Tulsa, Oklahoma for a camp meeting. At this time our oldest child was 16 and our youngest 7 years old. We were scheduled to be gone three days and the children were going to stay at home with our family checking in on them while we were out of town. After loading up the car, we gathered the children in the den and spoke a prayer of protection and wisdom over them and gave them a great big hug and kiss. Before we got into the car I heard the Holy Spirit say,

"Pray for the outside of the house, the outside structures, the neighborhood and occupants."

I thought I misunderstood what I had heard and said, "But we have already prayed for the children and the house. Did we miss something?"

Again, I heard the Holy Spirit repeat the request with the same wording. I glanced over at my husband and told him what I had just heard the Lord say and that we needed to do exactly what He has requested. So my husband and I got out of the car and stood in front of our house and prayed the prayer of protection, **in agreement with the will of God**, for the outside of our home its structure and all it contained. Then we turned towards the neighborhood and spoke a prayer of protection and agreement over it and all of the occupants and asked the Angels of the Lord to watch after all things of concern. I know we must have look foolish standing there speaking into the atmosphere, but we would have look more foolish if we had not obeyed the leading of the Holy Spirit.

Afterwards we got into the car and headed for Tulsa. As soon as we arrived at the hotel we took a nap before getting dressed for the evening service. We checked with the children before leaving the hotel and gave them all of our contact information and told them we would talk to them later. The camp meeting service that night was charged with the fire of the Holy Spirit and the speakers had just the words we needed to hear to recharge our spirits. We were so glad we had come and that the Lord had met us there. When we got back to the hotel we noticed there was a blinking light on the phone in our room. It was a message from the children to call them right away. My husband got the phone and called them immediately to ask if they were all right. This is the story they relayed to us:

Several hours after we had arrived in Tulsa, there was a commotion across the street from our house. There was a young man who lived there who was an acquaintance of my daughter. It was reported by the police that this young man was being harassed by several young men who followed him home and attacked him. Shots were fired from all parties spraying the neighborhood and our house with bullets. We were told the young man who lived at the residence was shot and later died. His mother, knowing I was a nurse, had run to our house banging at the door for assistance for her son, not knowing we were out of town. By the time the police got to the scene, the suspects were gone and the neighborhood in chaos. But this is the strange thing, our children slept through the entire situation. They were awakened by the police who were checking to see if they were all right. One policeman stated he had noticed a bullet hole in the window of our front room but there did not appear to be any damage to the house. Our children were considered to have been "lucky" they were not hurt. No one else in the neighborhood was hurt or their property damaged to our understanding.

Luck had nothing to do with the intervention of God. The Blessings of the Lord are made manifest through the power of the prayer of intercession. Right away I begin to think about all that could have happened if we had been there with them. I know my husband and I would have tried to stop the conflict, my daughter would have tried to help her friend and my son would have been in the window watching the whole matter go down. Although I am so sorry for the loss of life of that beautiful young man, I know things could have been so much worse if we had not listened to the voice of God and touched and agreed in prayer.

What I want to convey here is we did not know what we were praying for. The Holy Spirit did not reveal that part to us. But I am so thankful for being able to hear the voice of the Lord and having learned to obey him quickly and completely. As we have been teaching throughout this session, Our God is All Knowing, therefore He knows what we will need long before we need it. We must stop with the 50 questions and just trust and obey the one who has called and chosen us. The One who knows and declares our end from our beginning.

In Conclusion

Stay Focused!

And Jesus answered and said to them: "Take heed that no one deceives you.

Matthew 24:4

In this book I share a glimpse of the revelations and realities given to me regarding Our One and Only, Wise and True God. Even now, as I look through the pages, I see it is impossible to express who He is and what He does using earthly language. There are no words to convey my love for Him, for it deepens with each breath I take. What I do know is, I will seek Him the rest of my life and still not be satisfied until I can know Him as intimately as He knows me. Our Father wants us to search His depths. He promises He will be found of us, if we seek Him with all of our hearts. In our search for a closer relationship with Him we must not neglect the assignments and appointments He has set in place for us. We have work that must be done. There are those in darkness waiting for the light to come and reveal truth to them. To please the Lord, we must be about our Father's business. Falling by the wayside or becoming distracted is not an option. In closing, I believe it is imperative that I share with you a prophetic word I received while writing this book. But first I would like to share a spiritual encounter I received from God years ago that I believe was given for such a time as this.

Several years ago I received this open vision from the Lord and not until now have I received the interpretation.

After a difficult day at work, I rushed home to feed the family and afterwards went into the bedroom to pray. As was routine, I announced to my husband and children I would be praying and not to come into the room until I was finished. I shut the door to my room, turned out the lights, laid supine upon the bed and begin to talk to the Lord. Suddenly, I heard the Holy Spirit say, "Listen." As I listened, the Lord began to speak to me about certain issues I had before Him. He impressed upon me to listen to Him and not interrupt so I lay there quietly and attentively with my eyes closed. Before long I found myself resting in the Presence of the Lord as He instructed me in the word. Then I heard a knock at my door. I felt so good in His presence, I dare not break the connection to attend to carnal affairs, and therefore, I ignored the distraction believing, whoever it was, would soon go away. Seconds later, I heard my youngest child open the door and call my name. I ignored him and assumed when he saw me praying he would close the door and leave. Moments later I heard him walk to the foot of the bed and shake my foot. Annoyed, I sat up in the bed and began to chastise him for interrupting me, but when I open my eyes, no one was there.

I got up off the bed, check the bedroom door (which was still closed) and stepped out into the hallway only to realize it, too, was empty. Shaken, but not deterred, I again turned off the light, laid back on the bed and heard the Lord say, "Stay Focused." Trying not to think about what has just happened, I lay quietly and began to commune with God. After about 5 minutes there was another knock at the door. I thought about getting up to see if the children were playing a trick or game, but I refused to break my connection with God and just ignored the knock as before. Before long, I heard the door swing open and my daughter came into the room calling my name. Was this really happening . . . what was I to do? Then I felt her place her hand on my shoulder. As I reached to grab her hand, I opened my eyes and no one was there and the door remained closed.

*By this time I was ready to run from the room, but I heard
the Lord say once again, "Stay Focused." I laid back across
the bed, but by this time I was too upset to pray. Determined not
to allow fear to keep me from communing with the Lord, I soon
found myself closing my eyes and trying with all my might to get
back my connection with Him. It took a while before I was relaxed
enough to continue listening to His instructions to me, but just like
before He was able to put my mind at ease and calm me with His
presence. It was then that I heard Him say, "I need you to Stay
Focused." All of a sudden, I heard voices in the room and my bed
began to roll forward as though being pushed on to a freeway. I
heard the sound of cars passing by, horns blowing, lightning and
thunder sounded all around me. It was too much to bear. I jumped
out of bed, turned on the light, opened the door and ran from the
room. With tears running down my face I tried to explain to my
husband what had happened, but I had difficulty finding the words.
I felt like a failure because I allowed the things happening around
me to break my connection with God. I know enough about God
to know there was a lesson to be learned here, but I didn't fully
understand what it was until now.*

This is a corporate word from God to the Body of Christ:

**The Spirit of God speaks to the Church. He that has an ear to
hear, let him hear what the Spirit of the Lord is saying:**

**You have been called and chosen for a time such as this. I have
equipped you for the task ahead. You have everything you need to
fulfill the assignment. You have an enemy and its name is "distraction". The battlefield is your soul of emotions and decision
making. You are to stay focused on the task ahead and not be led
away by the issues, noises, voices and hype the enemy is sending
your way. This is a trick to cause you to be led astray on tangents
designed to corrupt and disillusion you. The louder the worldly**

issue; the easier it will be for you to lose focus. Jesus says, "I come that you might have life more abundantly." You are light and life. Share that light and life with those in darkness and the darkness will flee. Brace yourselves, for custom designed distractions will come. Your faith in My Omniscience and Omnipotence will be questioned. You will be tempted to see through the eyes of the flesh, but remember you are children of faith and not sight. Be not deceived, more is happening in the spiritual realm than you are aware. Satan knows his time is short. Don't allow yourselves to feed into the frenzy of the world's bright lights. Don't allow the squeaky wheels to take your attention off of the task at hand. Be about the work of the Kingdom of God. 'So do not worry or be anxious about tomorrow, for tomorrow will have worries and anxieties of its own. Sufficient for each day is its own trouble. But seek (aim at and strive after) first of all God's kingdom and His righteousness (His way of doing and being right), and then all these things, taken together, will be given you besides.' Matthews 6:33-34. Remember, My will shall stand. I will enjoy My good pleasure. My Word will guide you. Be filled with the Spirit – Lean not to your own understanding. Remember, the young are able to fight battles- I have ordained them as chosen deliverers. The battle is not over until the deliverance is complete and My Righteous Rule is restored.

I pray this book blesses you and increases your passion to search the depth of Father God. Remember the words God spoke in the beginning are still reverberating throughout time and space leading the way to our expected end. Our Father God's expectation of us is Great!

REFERENCES

Holy Bible New Living Translation (2nd ed.).(2008).Tyndale House Publishers,

Inc. Carol Stream, IL

KJV Super Giant Print Reference Bible (1996). Broadman & Holman Publishers.

Merriam-Webster's collegiate dictionary (2015). Springfield, MA: Merriam-Webster.

Rhodes, D. C. (2014). The Logos of the kingdom: A theological summary of God, his kingdom and his victorious church. Destiny Navigators, LLC. Decatur, GA

Webster's New World College Dictionary (4th ed.).(2004). Wiley Publishing, Inc.

Cleveland, OH

YouVersion Electronic Holy Bible (n.d.).Retrieved on July 27, 2015 from https://www.youversion.com